Praise for the *Voices of* Book Series

"Pure inspiration."

Shape Magazine

"...provides answers to practically anyone wondering 'What now?'...this worthy collection succeeds very well."

Publishers Weekly

"Hearing others' stories is the most substantial aspect of any support group... It's the universality of the emotions that links these essays and puts the human face on what can be a very scary disease. For all patient health collections."

Library Journal

Other Books by The Healing Project

WOMEN REINVENTED

WOMEN REINVENTED

True Stories of Empowerment and Change

Edited by
The Healing Project
www.thehealingproject.org
"Voices Of" Series Book No. 9

LaChance publishing

LACHANCE PUBLISHING • NEW YORK
www.lachancepublishing.com

All things have a beginning, although the journey from beginning to end is not always clear and straightforward. While work on *Voices Of* began just a short time ago, the seeds were planted long ago by beloved sources. This book is dedicated to Jennie, Larry, and Denise, who in the face of all things good and bad gave courage and support in excess. But especially to Richard, who taught us by the way he lived his life that anything is possible given enough time, hard work, and love.

Contents

PART ONE   Reclaiming Myself

PART TWO   Finding My Calling

PART THREE   Of Marriage and Motherhood

PART FOUR   My Spirit Renewed

The Healing Project

Debra LaChance

I wanted to ask the people around me, "Would you please raise your hand if you feel as isolated as I do?" Walking the busy streets of Manhattan on a beautiful sunny day, I was surrounded by people but I'd never felt so alone. Just minutes before, my doctors had broken the news to me that I had a particularly aggressive form of breast cancer.

Since moving to New York from a small town in Rhode Island, I'd had my share of ups and downs but had always risen to the challenges that living and working in New York can bring. But on this summer afternoon, I felt as if the world was suddenly rushing past me while I seemed to be moving in slow motion. I was completely alone.

After recovering from the initial shock, I found that one of the first things I almost automatically began to look for, besides doctors, was a sense of connection. I needed to hear from other people who had gone through what I was experiencing, who truly understood what it meant and who might be able to help. I wasn't ready for a regular support group, and with surgery and treatment looming, I simply didn't have the time. But I am an avid reader, and I assumed that finding the personal stories of those who had gone through this ordeal before me would be relatively easy. But there seemed to be a vacuum; almost nothing. Where were the real people to talk to? Where was the literature that wasn't just about the hardcore science of the disease, but about how to cope?

I knew there must be countless others out there who needed to tell their stories—and to hear the stories of others as well. My thoughts kept returning to that walk through Manhattan after I'd heard my diagnosis, and that feeling of terrible loneliness. As sympathetic as friends and loved ones could be, I felt that no one could truly understand this journey except someone who had made it before. I was convinced that getting and giving courage, comfort, and strength were as important as good medical care, and I became determined to help build a community for people like me who were undergoing the terribly isolating experience of dealing with a life-threatening or chronic disease.

My cancer diagnosis was indeed a defining moment in my life, and out of it The Healing Project was born. The Healing Project's mission is to become a bridge across which people can make those all-important emotional connections. I began to develop The Healing Project as a place where people can contribute funds for research, time for connecting with others, and most of all, a place to share their stories. Since then, The Healing Project has been collecting stories for books like this one: books that inspire and inform for the road ahead and impart a sense of community for those caught up in dealing with the moment.

You'll find many defining moments in *Women Reinvented*. It's our hope that this volume will strike a chord with women who have found themselves at a crossroads, be it emotional, professional, physical or spiritual. We all have decisions to make about the direction of our lives, and it can be comforting and rewarding to read how other women have dealt with the challenges—and opportunities—that life can offer.

There's so much strength to be found in the voices of others, and I hope you enjoy these stories by and of remarkable women who have so much wisdom to share.

Debra LaChance is the creator and founder of The Healing Project.

Foreword

Courtney E. Martin

When I was 24 years old, fresh out of graduate school and flummoxed about how my life was really going to work, my mom gave me a dog-eared copy of Mary Catherine Bateson's *Composing a Life*. At first, I was skeptical. After all, it had first been published in a time when shoulder pads and jazzercise were popular. It was 2004, and I was just squeaking past my rebel-against-everything-my-mom-tells-me phase in life. This didn't seem promising.

In spite of myself, I cracked the book open one long Saturday afternoon in Brooklyn, and discovered that, once again, my mom had earned herself a major "I told you so" moment. The book is, as the author herself puts it, "a study of five artists engaged in that act of creation that engages us all—the composition of our lives." Bateson examines the daily rituals, choices, adventures, challenges, and celebrations that make up five fascinating women's lives from an anthropological perspective—looking for both the implicit and explicit values, the marks of the personal and the political, the lessons about power and happiness.

I was stunned, simply stunned. You see, as much as I knew—deep down—that my mom's life was important, I had never seen it reflected in literature. As much as I intuited that it was the practices and preferences of my aunts, my female teachers, my older friends, my mentors that were teaching me the most, I had never considered them "legitimate" sites of study. Instead, I'd spent four years at an Ivy League college, intimidated by all the know-it-all men in my classes, all the know-it-all men in the books I read, all the know-it-all men who authored those books. They seemed unconcerned with the daily lives of women. Deep down I knew they were wrong, that they were missing out on one of the richest resources for wisdom about invention and reinvention. But I also didn't have the confidence to own that intuition.

In Bateson's groundbreaking book, she essentially said to all women, *Your lives are art. They are worthy of witnessing.* It was not a small revelation for me. In fact, I've spent the next ten years of my life writing, largely, about women's lives. I follow in the footsteps of Mary Catherine Bateson in an attempt to watch and listen to women, and write it all down, so that we all might find ourselves reflected in literature, appreciated, valued, and legitimized in the public sphere.

About a half a dozen years later, I broke open *Women Reinvented: True Stories of Empowerment and Change* and spent another Saturday afternoon — still in Brooklyn — stunned by the beauty, power, and necessity of women's stories. Within these pages, Mary Catherine Bateson's project of witnessing and honoring the profundity of women's choices lives on — this time in a rich, personal essay format that is relatable, courageous, devastating, and inspiring.

This volume speaks to such a vast diversity of women, inventing and reinventing themselves in the most surprising and brave ways. There is something exquisitely extraordinary in the ordinariness of it all — loving and losing, birthing and mourning, surviving illness and purposelessness, finding a small voice inside that urges forward movement, that believes in the power of tragedy to sow the seeds of triumph. These women come from all over the country. They come from all kinds of economic and geographic situations. They officiate weddings, coordinate volunteers, fish, conduct research, practice law, parent, teach, garden. They expose their lives in inspired prose in order to find meaning in their own journeys, and in acts of true generosity, to help us find meaning in our own.

Contributor Susannah Risley sums up the wisdom in this volume quite distinctly: "I was broken hearted, jammed up, fogged in, but not crazy. I could tell the difference." The women's stories in this book help us, the readers, tell that same difference. Their words help us know that even as we may feel broken, alone, beyond repair, we are actually just becoming something more. As Pema Chodron, Buddhist teacher and the quintessential artist of life reinvention, writes, "we can endure a lot of pain and pleasure for the sake of finding out who we are and what this world is, how we tick and how our world ticks, how the whole thing just *is*."

These women have endured. And now they are here to paint pictures of that instructive enduring. As contributor Bobbi Arduini writes, "My mom and I discover that we both like to garden. I tell my mother about naming all the trees when I was a kid and we both cry a little, because even though we lived together, we still missed so much of each other." I think that women continue to exist in a sort of tender and strangely disconnected space, where we miss too much of each other in our dogged pursuit of the individual, successful female life — or at the very least, the appearance of one. Like Bobbi and her mother, we have to slow down, name the trees, acknowledge our sadness, and forge new friendships, cemented by honest, beautiful storytelling. This volume is another beginning.

Courtney E. Martin is the award-winning author of *Perfect Girls, Starving Daughters: How the Quest for Perfection is Harming Young Women*. She is a senior correspondent for *The American Prospect Online* and her work has appeared in the *Washington Post, Newsweek,* and the *Christian Science Monitor,* among others. She has appeared on *Good Morning America, The TODAY Show, The O'Reilly Factor* and MSNBC, and has spoken on radio programs and at colleges, non-profits, and parenting organizations. In addition, Courtney consults with social justice organizations throughout the nation, including the Ms. Foundation for Women, the National Council for Research on Women and the Bartos Institute for the Constructive Engagement of Conflict.

Acknowledgments

This book would not have been possible without the selfless dedication of many people giving freely of their valuable time and expertise. We would particularly like to thank Courtney E. Martin for lending her extraordinary expertise and insight; Susanne Van Cleave Sharp and Gloria Monti, Ph.D. for assisting in the selection of the contributors; and the many people who contributed their stories to us, for their courage, their generosity and their humanity.

WOMEN REINVENTED

PART ONE

———————

Reclaiming Myself

A Letter of Thanks to My Rapist

Elizabeth Tissot

I am reluctant to write about you raping me. Rape is the type of thing that puts people so very on edge; edge of their seats, clinging to the edge, need a drink to take the edge off kind of edge.

Before you raped me, I was vibrant in the worst kind of way. I moved like I was a dancer and danced like I was terrible in bed. But I was not a walking contradiction, because to say that would be cliché, and I was no cliché.

It's true that most of the time I was being watched, a little shining speck in the middle of a sea of black umbrellas and suits, a speck that was undeniably seen. If you were looking at something special then, something that seemed to rise to the top in a bubble, then you may have been staring at me. I wonder now if you chose me for this reason.

Those days, before you raped me, I had a smell so very few ever forgot although they never even really knew it. I left my scent wherever I went, my bakery-sweet sweat to linger in white cotton curtains that blew in gusts, in silk tablecloths spoiled with red wine, sheets dirty with sex juice. It was a scent that reminded people of the *worst* kind of girl, one who lies and cheats and has found the perfect rhythm in the swing of her gait—because she's figured out the power of her own hips. It was this scent that allowed me to attract and collect people like flies to sticky paper. Then I'd disappear. No warnings, no letters. Nothing at all.

Elizabeth Tissot

That is how it was with me, then. In time they would all get over it, like a death or a birth or all those things that happen in between, but every so often a gust of wind would pass, or a fork would drop to the floor, and it would somehow stir up a memory of me that they thought had settled. An atom of me, a fraction of a drop of my sweet sweat would soar again suddenly and then drift, finally settling on a hair right inside their nose. And it would be enough to make them blow up, it would be enough to make them throw up, it would be enough to make them get up and leave. It would be enough to make them stay and keep sniffing around for more.

That was all I was then. A vibrant, shining speck with no purpose. People were consumed by me for no reason that I could ever fully understand, and still don't. Maybe it was the way my eyes always burned brighter than others because I had just been crying, or the way my lips swelled up like an erection, because I had just been biting them in a fit of nerves. I like to think that people did not know these things about me, but they must have. I sense that's why they were drawn to me, because they wanted to swoop down like a real life angel and heal the pretty and delicate girl that I was. They wanted to change me, to reset me, like an out of place bone that only needed the most expert hands to jostle it back into its socket. Everybody likes to be a savior.

I so wish this is where we could leave me. A vibrant, sweetly-scented and sad speck. But things just got so much worse once I started having panic attacks all the time. They unraveled my life and left me in their wake. With every attack I was sure I would die; stroke out, burst an aneurysm, hyperventilate a coronary wall to its limit. At times they would fill me with such a profound fear that I would pass out and not come to for hours. I assumed the role of a dead woman walking, and started drinking all the time — mostly the hard stuff. I was always lonely but too fragile to pick up the phone, and much too ill to remove myself from the apartment — ever. I puked daily into a paper wastebasket that was permanently stationed below the foot of my bed, next to the balled up tissues soggy with tears that collected on my floor. I chain-smoked and had a death rattle cough that was enough to drive anyone away, not that anyone came around anymore, anyway.

Except that group of kids had moved down the hall a few weeks before. They drank and smoked and rarely left the building. And that was our one common link: that we'd become unlinked from everything else. Soon we were passing out together regularly. They appreciated my records and couches and I appreciated the fact that I didn't need to remember their names for them to keep on coming. I think they left the door unlocked most nights, and I think that you knew this. I couldn't help it, though; I was always the first to bed.

There I would lie amid magazines and wing-eared books, and my laptop at the edge, always powered on and humming with guilt. I lay in fetal position all day and all night, under my dirt and whiskey-stained down comforter, usually tearing up because I was always just *that near the edge*. I wasn't a vibrant speck anymore. I no longer believed in anything, and felt slighted or wronged. I was convinced that I was a victim of my own genes, because my father had two sisters who corkscrewed out of control and killed themselves at my age, and my mother's side had liver failure and multiple DUI tickets.

> "There is a way to stir, that pushes you to the edge, that brings forth a glow that you can't get from a bottle, or a sermon, or people who try to convince you they know more."

And these are things you never knew about me. The place where you left me, sweating and exposed on top of my sheets, was not where you intended to leave me, I think. You thought you had the power to make a victim out of me, but in my mind, I already was one. It was never possible to make me feel any lower than I already did, don't you see? You derailed my life, and I have to show you in some way what that means to me. I want to tell you our story, a story of how you tried to make a mess of me, but saved me instead. A story of how you rolled through my life like a tornado and shook me so violently that I was ejected out of the pile of shit I was living in and landed down to where I am now.

I remember exactly what I did after it happened. I stood up out of bed, and taking on the voice of a man reciting figures in a business meeting for some important accounting firm, calmly asked you to leave. I wasn't afraid, because in my head I was mentally fingering the dull side of a blade in my kitchen, or the scored button of the can of mace I had stashed under my bed. And it was odd to me, the way you spoke so coolly. You asked me if you could stay until your "buds" got there, and I told you no, that you could not stay, and that was that. I played the game with you, and I was good. Of course, you had no idea then that you would spend the rest of your life in jail, or how short, even, the rest of your life would be.

While you gathered up all of your street-stained clothes and headed for my door, I stayed in bed frozen; except for my lips, which were smacking and sticking together nervously. The heat was violent, and a pool of sweat had formed inside my bellybutton.

Lying in the damp heat that flooded my crappy studio apartment, I focused not on what you had just done to me but on the mess that was my life. You were still making your way out; you walked so slowly, stepping over bodies, which were everywhere. Drunken bodies that would not wake, even while you were raping me, though you must have been grunting. "Pale Blue Eyes'" was on repeat, and television light and murky ice cream spoons polluted the room.

When I finally heard the rickety slam of you leaving through my front door, I calmly pulled my hair into a knot and stood up out of bed. My first thought was to locate my dogs, and I remember finding them huddled together in the closet, eyes squeezed shut as if something had happened to their mother that they didn't want to see. But they were there, and they were real and they were safe, so I was thankful.

Next, I walked into to the bathroom, where I peed and flicked the sleep out of my eyes. My boxers were still pulled down, exposing my underwear just a bit, and I left them that way. The lights were dim in there, and I closed the curtain carefully and checked my body for bruising or abrasions, using the glow of my cell phone to guide me.

After completing what was, to me, a satisfactory exam, I stumbled into the kitchen to find some paper and pen. I say stumbled not because I was terrified of you, but because my stuff was everywhere, just the way I liked it. And when I finally found the back of some stupid crumbled-up receipt, I took a dog-chewed sharpie from the nearest drawer and made a list, like this:

1. Right upper quadrant of the torso: two dime-sized bruises forming, possibly fingerprints. New.

2. Left lateral scraping on the posterior of the right thigh. Possibly new.

3. Prominent bruising on the proximodistal axis of the right knee. Old—please disregard.

See? You barely even left a mark. I still tell people, "If you've got to get raped, get it the way it happened to me." Not once did you threaten me with a knife to the neck, nor did you inflict much pain on my body at all. When it was over, you acted as if it were the end of a date: "I'll see you around," you told me. I was hardly conscious, anyway. My mind must've been protecting me by not allowing me to wake up, by putting me in a sort of sleep paralysis. And I am so thankful for this, constantly wondering how things would have been if I had been awake. Surely I would have tried to fight you off while you were inside me, while you were so worked up. It would've pissed you off and I could have been badly injured, or worse, dead.

Though the list largely ignored the most obvious areas of impact, I was wary of touching my insides. Your evidence was in there, and I didn't want to screw with it. I was a prudent person, who was going to do all of the things any prudent person would do after something like this. I was going to collect evidence, make lists, and gather my sheets into a securely fastened garbage bag. My clothing, I would keep on. I was told I was supposed to. See, at this point you probably thought I would be like the rest of your victims and keep quiet. You didn't know it yet, but I would soon ruin your life, and after that, it would be *my* fault that you were killed.

I remember being irritated that it was only 4:30 A.M. Most people were sleeping soundly, or waking up to run off to their work at some factory. Lovers still in their honeymoon phase were rousing each other for sex. I cursed you then for leaving me with all of this shit to deal with. I wanted to stay in bed lazily and throw my dogs bones. I wanted to stay in that apartment forever and never leave until I was carried out on a stretcher. This was not because of you, though. I am not one to give credit where credit's not due.

What happened next is probably not important to you. I'm sure you know the drill—you've done this before. I followed all of the procedures and guidelines that anyone in my situation is supposed to follow. You didn't expect that, did you? And I am only telling you the following things because I want you to know that you didn't ruin my morning completely.

The cops that picked me up were young and Italian and good looking, and when I made jokes about you raping me, they politely laughed. I tell you this because I want you to know that you did not leave me completely broken like you wanted me to be. I told them that you must've been small down there, because it hardly even hurt. I enjoyed speaking of you this way. We stopped at Starbucks, and they paid for my Mocha.

It was interesting to see the anatomy of my insides blown up on a large screen. Because of you, I found out that my cervix was perfect, delicately curved in all of the right places and colored pink like a baby rosebud. My uterus was slightly longer than normal, which would make pregnancy easier on me in the future, and would reduce the risk of stretch marks. The doctors that performed my exam also told me that if they could choose any victim's insides to showcase in a remake of any classical human anatomy book, they would choose mine. All of these things because of you, and I brag about them to this day.

To think of what happened next still makes me angry and a bit sick to my stomach. The way that you involved my mother makes me want to bury you alive. This is the part of our story that is the most dark; rough around the edges and so very lonely and cold. It is the part of our story that I want to keep as far away from as possible.

It must've taken forty rings for my mom to answer, when I called her. She was six hours away in San Francisco, and it was still so early. When she finally picked up the phone, I assumed the voice of someone who was newly broken. Because I thought that's what would be expected of me. When I told her that you raped me, I could *hear* her face turn rice-paper white, and any trace of sleep she still held onto immediately slipped away from her. She said she would drive up right away, and she spoke of renting us a beautiful hotel room to stay in until all of this was sorted out. You killed a part of my mother that day, and for this, I will never forgive you.

And my biggest fear then was what I was going to say to her and all of these well-intentioned people when they arrived. I knew that they would want there to be tears, for me to well up right in front of them and beg for help. I dreaded the dead air and smoothing of non-wrinkled pants on laps. I dreaded the moment when I would finally clear my throat to speak. That moment would be the only invitation they needed, and they would all whip their heads in my direction, simulta-neously, as if this one sound just might be the start of a quivering retelling. People... they can surprise you. The first person I saw after you raped me was my future roommate, an Asian entertainment agent who had an "I'm obviously gay but I'll never admit it" way about him. He was the only person who answered my calls because he was the only person awake, my only friend with an adult job. When he first walked into the Rape Center and saw me, he playfully asked me if I was audi-tioning for "Monster II." This meant something to us because I had finally showered and my hair had air dried like shit straw, making me look like a frailer version of Charlize Theron's character in the original.

Later, he drove me to one of my favorite places, a tacky chain-buffet, the kind that you aren't normally supposed to go to in Los Angeles. He forced me to eat the crusts of his pizza, and once I did, he drove me to his apartment. I fell asleep on his couch watching some comforting eighties movie, and dreamed of my mom's arrival, of her checking us both into some fabulous hotel. I dreamed of an overstuffed bed and pay-per-view movies.

I woke up a few hours later to my mom at his door, looking more beau-tiful than she should have for the amount of worry she'd been through and the hours of sleep you had robbed her of. I was tired and delirious, and she picked my body up and carried me to her car. And I can still picture it so vividly, this five foot-four, rail-thin woman carrying her five foot-ten daughter with barely an ounce of effort. I slept in her car, corpse-like, as she scanned the highway for hotels. Her modest Honda felt richer than it ever had, and all I wanted was to be an infant again and to be forever nestled against her breast. Writing this, I am tearing up, and the thought of my wonderful mother sleeping a few rooms away is almost too much for me to bear. I want to run to her and lie with her this very instant, to hold her forever and tell her how much she means to me.

I want you to think of this now. Think of my mother who loves me with everything while you are loved by no one and nothing. Think of our embrace now, as you lie in some shallow and unmarked grave, absent of visitors.

Once we found a hotel that allowed dogs, we checked in and waited for the LAPD to call us. I was aware that I would have to identify you from a picture book, and I knew it wouldn't be hard. You were lacking in height and whale-like in weight. I would know your shit-grin anywhere.

After my mother had sat in bed with me for hours watching true crime TV shows and eating Italian takeout, the cops arrived with four large binders. And there were so many people in that book who looked just like you. But you—you were on the first page, and like I said: I'd know that shit-grin anywhere. After I pointed to your bloated face, and told them that you were the one who raped me, the cops said they could pick you up right then, right there. Because, my darling rapist, you must not have been very bright. You had such a colorful rap sheet, and you always got caught.

Later in life, after I put you in jail and you somehow made bail, I found out that you had gotten yourself killed in a drive-by. You were there on the street by my apartment for almost a full day before you were found, your brains spilling out of you and settling underneath your head like some sick sort of pillow. I heard that you were there to see me, to punish me for "telling on you." So it was me, surely, that indirectly *killed you*. Think of this irony now, and let it sit with you.

And thinking back, you weren't even a mistake at all. If you were a mistake, I would obsess and would want to know more. I would want to know if there were pain or tears when you were shot, and how it felt to be alone on the dirty streets of Hollywood with your insides pooled around you. I would want to know how it felt to be dying and alone, with all of your "friends" miles away, terrified of being sent back to where you all came from. If you were a mistake, if your raping me was a mistake, I might have stayed until someone came to take you away on a stretcher. I would have cared. I would've wanted you to live, to stick around so I could find out *why*. But I've left you there, a bad accident and a mess, like you always were.

I thank you, despite all of the things you did to me. I thank you for putting your disgusting 3-incher inside of me. I thank you for giving me that extra push I needed to hit rock bottom. Without you, I would never have been able to climb back out of where I was. After you raped me, I had no idea how to be the girl I was that night, the girl I was before you did it. A part of me died that morning, yeah. But it wasn't in the way that most people who are raped die. You did not kill some shiny and glad part of me and turn me into a victim. What you did to me was so detestable and horrible that it brought my life to the lowest level of low, and I finally had the ending I needed to close that utterly pathetic chapter of my life. You ended the book, finally. You've written the Cliff Notes, even.

Because of you, I have learned that it is possible to find *some kind* of God. And I don't care what people say. There is a way to stir, that pushes you to the edge, that brings forth a sort of glow that you can't get from a bottle, or a sermon, or people who try to convince you they know more.

You have revitalized me. You have saved me. You have resurrected the vibrant speck that I used to be. You gave me a purpose, and for that, I thank you.

Elizabeth Tissot is a former fashion model and current prelaw student. She lives in San Francisco with two dogs and a cat, all of which were rescued from Los Angeles pounds. When not busy with her studies, she writes and sings the blues in two local bands.

Brenda Martin, Who Do You Think You Are?

Brenda Martin

I don't like to remember the past. I guess it seems no less tragic today than it did when my family and I were living it, in the housing projects next to the Brooklyn Navy Yard. We spent ten long years there, surviving the gritty, cracked concrete streets haunted by drug addicts, where the blood of murdered teenage boys seeped and disappeared.

I was in the midst of transformation then, in an awkward, painful, laborious trudge up what seemed like an impossible mountain. In those days, every strained breath was a prayer that someday my struggle might mean something, that one day living wouldn't be so hard. This journey had started at the very bottom.

"Who do you think you are?"

Daddy would often demand this of me, his soured, red-rimmed eyes ablaze with fury. He felt victorious when I cringed. At least through the power of his large fists, he had control.

"Who do you think you are?"

It was a drunken plea for me to remember my origins: an abandoned baby girl born in 1951 in Chicago to an emotionally impaired mother only thirteen years older than me. A lonely child passed from relative to relative. A naïve nineteen year-old who, by the summer of 1970, had given birth to two illegitimate daughters.

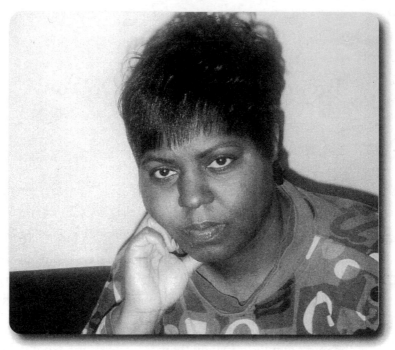

Brenda Martin

My thirteen-year union with the father would produce three more illegitimate children and a well-practiced tendency to cringe when I heard loud noises, my frazzled senses preparing for the violence to come. As far as everyone was concerned, the verdict was in: A welfare mom with five children. Brenda Martin wouldn't amount to anything.

"Who do you think you are?"

I asked the question myself in 1984 when, after bouts of homelessness, hunger and shame, I walked into New York City Technical College and came out with an application packet. That year, my first daughter entered high school and I, with my two young sons still in elementary school and a toddler clinging to my skirt, entered college. It's funny, but when I was younger, I had pictured myself going there. I didn't know how I could or if I would, but somehow I did.

Taking on a full load of science and math courses while doing the work-study program and raising five children was no easy feat. I often fell asleep at the kitchen table, my cheek flat against the open page of my book. "Don't ask me to go to bed," I'd tell the children. "I have to study."

The fact that I was working myself to the bone was hardly consolation to the man of the house. He didn't like it. Maybe he was frightened by the new determination in my eyes. My newfound confidence drove me to push harder, study longer, to get good grades. My burgeoning pride in myself and my ability to save my family from poverty made him feel like I was somehow mocking him, calling him less than a man.

One night, in a drunken rage, he chased me down a flight of steps. I fell and broke my leg in three places. Afterwards, I often sat at the kitchen table, my leg encased in a cast past my thigh, with my chemistry and algebra books open before me. I would imagine the classes that I was missing and would weep softly to myself. I missed an entire semester of school because of this injury.

> "I had an inner yearning that craved to be satisfied. I thirsted for dignity, for independence and most certainly, for the right to live without fear."

But I didn't give up. I couldn't; I felt that my family's safety and my own depended on it. I eventually graduated with an Associates degree in applied science and instantly went from welfare mom to working mom. In fact, I worked three jobs. It was exhausting, but I was consumed with determination to provide for us and save money. I was still climbing the mountain. Some nights I'd have to walk home past the Fort Greene projects, which had a very high murder rate.

In the meantime, this motherless, fatherless girl who had never felt loved enough was rapidly changing and evolving. My mate had been right to fear the newfound look of self-determination in my eyes. In my struggle for education and opportunity, I also had an inner yearning that craved to be satisfied. I thirsted for dignity, for independence and most certainly, for the right to live without fear. He eventually left, and died soon after. I still flinched in my sleep at the slightest sound, and I'd wake in a panic. It would take years to lose that habit.

There was a nursing program for hospital employees at Staten Island College. It was a competitive program with only a limited number of spaces, but I got in. By this time, I had managed to save enough money to buy a car. After a lifetime of sweltering subways and freezing bus stops, a car was no less fantastic than a magic carpet. But I was still working very hard: full-time at Brooklyn Hospital, part-time at another hospital while also being a full-time nursing student at Staten Island College.

The hard work eventually paid off, and it was with tremendous pride that I was able to move my family out of the projects. I'll never forget the day we moved. I stood near the entryway of our building, where the summer sun was barely able to steal in between the iron patchwork bars that decorated the entry. A neighbor stood next to me, watching the procession of people and furniture, his solemn gaze straight ahead. "Congratulations," he said.

We moved to a rented two family home on a quiet, tree-lined street in Staten Island. It felt like waking up from a terrible dream. Soon after that, I graduated from the nursing program as a licensed registered nurse. It was a victory that felt like everyone's victory. Because of this accomplishment, a few relatives and friends were inspired to go to school themselves.

I was very proud to receive the Nurse of Distinction Award, and I went on to purchase a two-story home in the Port Richmond neighborhood in Staten Island. After so many years of struggle, I finally achieved the

American Dream. Little Brenda Martin, who had borne two kids by the time she was nineteen, was the first to graduate from college and the first homeowner in our extended family.

I think it is the knowledge of the past that drives me, as a psychiatric nurse, to reach out to my patients, to love them and accept them unconditionally. When they come to me, they are at their lowest: vulnerable, shaken and broken, confused, defiant. But from my own experience I can see in all of them something that lies within the hearts of every human being: the desire to be loved.

Looking back on what I've been able to accomplish against tough odds, I think of the question that was asked so long ago:

"Brenda Martin, who do you think you are?"

And I think I can answer that. I am a woman, born into poverty to a thirteen-year-old girl, with no father, passed from relative to relative. A woman who fought not just for an education, not just for her self-respect, not just for her children's sake, but for her purpose. I am a woman who believes that nothing is unsalvageable. That anything is possible.

Born in Chicago, Illinois and raised in Chicago and Brooklyn, New York, Brenda Martin currently lives in Staten Island, New York. She enjoys traveling on vacations and spending time with her grandchildren.

Leaving

Sue Sanders

I was resting on the metal hospital bed, exhausted, slick with sweat and happier than I'd ever been, finally holding in my arms the baby I'd carried inside me for the last nine months. My reverie was broken when my husband murmured, "She spoke to me."

He meant it literally.

I looked up from our newborn, Elizabeth, who wasn't saying anything but was foraging unsuccessfully for my breast. What was he talking about? Our daughter was many months away from attempting her first word, much less stringing them together in a sentence. But John was serious. I studied his eyes. They were wider than they should've been, his pupils as big as our newborn's palms.

He was off his medication again. I turned away from his psychotic eyes to my daughter's murky, bluish gray ones. She was perfect. I kissed the top of her head, tasting the dampness of her dark newborn hair. I gently placed my hand over her smooth back, her body smaller than some of the stuffed toys that waited for her in her newly-painted room. I pushed John's words out of my mind. He'd go back on his meds. We had a baby. He'd be a good father.

For the last few years, John had been slipping and sliding in and out of bipolar episodes. When he'd take his medicine, he'd change back into the man I knew, the man I'd fallen in love with fifteen years earlier.

Sue Sanders

But he'd only be fine for a little while—until he stopped taking his pills. Although he hadn't stayed on his meds in the past for himself or for me, I was certain he'd stay on them now for our daughter. I don't know if I held tight to my denial because something deep inside of me was too terrified even to think about being on my own with a young child, but it never occurred to me to leave him—divorce was something that happened to other people, not to us. So as I'd promised in my vows, I stayed, through his sickness and his sporadic health. Over the past five years ignoring the reality of my situation had somehow become second nature. Wishful thinking was as self-aware as I got—if I closed my eyes and believed hard enough that John could change, I just knew that he would. Or so I told myself.

I begged him to see a doctor and he refused, or he'd go once or twice and then abruptly end treatment. I pleaded with him to take his medicine and he assured me he would, but when I locked myself in the bathroom and counted the blue pills in the amber bottles, it was clear he was lying.

Now that I was a mother, I had other things to worry about and I kept myself busy with my daughter so I wouldn't have to think about anything else. The first months were a blur of diaper changes, nursing, lullabies and cuddling. I took walks with Elizabeth snuggled next to me in her baby carrier. I held her close and watched as she nursed, her eyes fluttering as sleep overtook her, a thin thread of milk dripping down her cheek. I'd study her as she napped in my arms so I could memorize every bit of her babyhood. John was uninterested. Most of the time he was upstairs—I could hear him moving furniture in his office for reasons known only to him. I closed my mind to what was happening overhead and hummed a melody to my napping baby.

Elizabeth grew and changed before my eyes. She became too big for the backward-facing newborn carrier and now faced forward, trying out her new toothy smile at everyone we passed on our frequent neighborhood strolls. My husband grinned too, a mask of normalcy but with eyes that were glazed and as difficult for me to read as Sanskrit. He went on and off his meds and, when on, was more like his old self, but when off—which was far more often—he became someone I didn't know. When I woke up each morning, I was never sure who he'd be that day: the man I fell in love with or a stranger in the grip of manic psychosis.

For Elizabeth's first birthday party, both sets of grandparents came over and sang while Elizabeth sat in her highchair smearing chocolate frosting on the tray, flinching slightly at the surprising coldness of her first taste of ice cream. John, though physically there, seemed far away. A month later we went to my in-laws' house for dinner. John, normally as docile as a butterfly, tussled with his father over his car keys, muttering that he had to get away. While his mother took Elizabeth into another room, pretending all was fine, I locked myself into the bathroom with the phone, and dialed 911. He was taken away by the police, who attempted to calm him. He argued and pleaded with them that he was okay. But he wasn't—he was rushed to a psychiatric hospital. The morning after his first night in the hospital, Elizabeth peered under her father's pillow, asking "Da?" as if he'd shrunk and could be found under it. Though she seemed to wonder where he went, she didn't seem to miss him. During those two weeks he was in the hospital, Elizabeth learned to walk and proudly tottered around when we visited him, which we did regularly. He was released when his insurance ran out and, when he came home, he still wasn't well.

I tried to pretend he was, though. I was as good as my daughter was— perhaps even better—at imaginary play. Instead of dressing in tulle gowns and glittery wings, I'd put on a smiling face, telling myself John would get better—that he'd realize he was sick. I'd make excuses to friends about missing their children's birthday parties. I told my daughter her father couldn't go with us to the zoo because he'd been up late working. I lied to myself that John was fine, that all families had issues and that he'd be okay soon. We lived like this for the next few years until my daughter woke me up.

> "I slowly began to peel off all the layers of denial, guilt, and sadness. Underneath I discovered something I didn't expect: I was far stronger than I thought I was."

Spring seemed to come from nowhere after the long, bleak New York winter. It was a perfect day for a picnic in Prospect Park. John had decided he'd come with us and I was glad, as we hadn't done anything as a family in a long time. And although he'd been racing toward another full-blown manic episode, staying out all night, spending money we didn't have on clothes he didn't need, maybe getting out of the apartment and into the sunshine was just what he needed.

Families filled the park, lured by the first perfect Saturday of spring. I spread the blanket on a patch of grass in the sun, near a budding tree. She ran toward John, holding out her arms to him. He stayed as still as the statue we'd passed at the park's perimeter. Before her face fell, I held out my arms and she flung herself into mine. John stared straight ahead at something in the distance. Elizabeth called, "Daddy, play ball." John, seeming not to hear, got up and walked away. I tried to salvage our picnic, but it was ruined.

That night, after she'd splashed in the bath, I tucked her into bed. "I don't like daddy really much," she said quietly. I didn't know what to say. It occurred to me that I had been desperately trying to hold my dream of a family together for myself, not necessarily thinking about what was best for my daughter. But our nuclear family had detonated and I needed to protect my child from the shrapnel. I brushed a blonde curl from her eyes.

"He loves you very much, but he's sick," I said, feeling like I was fibbing, and wondered if it was as apparent to my daughter as it was to me. I honestly didn't know what John thought and who he loved. I think it was his illness, as he'd gone off his meds yet again, choosing his sickness over our family's health. She looked up at me and snuggled into my arm. I suddenly knew that whatever happened with John, the two of us would be okay.

A few days later, John was hospitalized again. We visited him in the hospital and I told him if he got help, stayed in the hospital, and took his pills, we would be there for him. He checked himself out a few days later. My daughter and I left.

Sometimes it takes a life-shattering event to force a person into action. Underneath the sadness I felt, there was a more powerful sensation: relief. I'd tried for so long to make the marriage work on my own that I never realized how exhausted I was until it was over. On my first day as a single mom, I pushed my daughter's stroller through a street fair on Brooklyn's Fifth Avenue. I felt lighter than I had in years — so weightless, in fact, that I held more tightly to the stroller's handle, just to be sure I wouldn't float away. I grasped it when Elizabeth hopped out and pogoed to the music of a local punk rock band, on a small stage behind giant speakers. Elizabeth seemed as happy and free as I realized I now felt.

Yes, I cried after I put my daughter to bed that night, and many other nights, but I was mourning a relationship that was long gone. I wasn't able to change my ex, but I could transform my life—for myself and for my daughter.

After I left John, I was kick-started into finally making adjustments to my life, and discovered how truly wonderful it felt to *do* rather than wait and have things done to me. After we left John, I slowly began to peel off all the layers of denial, guilt, and sadness that I'd let build up over 18 years. Underneath I discovered something I didn't expect: I was far stronger than I thought I was, and I deserved happiness. The big change suddenly led to a million smaller transformations: over the next couple of years I joined a food co-op, took my daughter to Paris, started a single moms' group, taught English to foreign adults, took chances and met someone, got married, and started writing.

Sometimes I think about what my life would have been like if I'd stayed with John. But I can't even imagine it. Because I am not that woman.

Sue Sanders is a writer living in New Patlz, New York. Her essays have appeared in *Redbook* and *Parents* and a variety of other parenting and lifestyle magazines. An essay about her first date in nineteen years is included in the anthology *Ask Me About My Divorce: Women Open Up About Moving On* (Seal Press, June 2009).

The Upward Turn

Elissa L. Perry

I leaned across the table, smiled a flirtatious smile, cocked my head and asked with feigned surprise, "Are you looking down my blouse?" He was clearly flustered, but before he could answer I said, "You can, I don't mind."

Ten minutes later when we left the dimly lit wine bar, a man shouted some indecipherable words of encouragement, acknowledging that what he had just witnessed was the beginning of something new.

Tom and I walked arm-in-arm, dodging raindrops, until we found a brightly-lit hotel awning. We needed shelter from the rain so that we could kiss—furtively, passionately, awkwardly, unsure of where it would lead. The desk clerk came out from behind his station to tell us we had to move along. Yes, it was official: I was now acting like a teenager.

We rounded the corner and found another patch of city wall to lean against. His hands made their way down the back of my fashionably tight jeans. He stopped kissing me to remark, more than pleasantly surprised, "Oh Professor, you're wearing thong underwear."

Yes, in fact the very pair of hot pink thong underwear that my mother-in-law had given me a year earlier on my birthday, as a sort of pick-me-up gift. I rarely wore thong underwear, and when I did it was to avoid unsightly lines—to avoid stares, not to encourage them. This evening

Elissa L. Perry

was different. Tonight, in my hot pink thong underwear, I felt desired and sensuous; Tom was helping me think about myself in new and different ways. Tonight, Tom was breathing new life into me.

Two years earlier, I'd had the life sucked out of me. It was a sunny day. I walked toward the subway, talking to my husband, my cell phone pressed to my ear. Phil was athletic, fit and handsome. But on that day he wasn't feeling well. He had left work early. He'd been vomiting and was sitting on a bench outside his office. He said he'd make his way home when he felt better. An hour and a half later, I got a phone call I never could have imagined receiving. Phil had collapsed. I heard the words "in the field," "ER," "critical condition."

And then I was in a cold, cheerless emergency room watching my husband die, listening to the monotone sound the heart monitor makes when the line goes flat. Because my husband's heart had stopped. Just like that. At 10:35 P.M., just five hours after we spoke on the phone, Phil was dead. There was no clear medical explanation why. I had lost the person with whom I had the deepest personal connection—the person who knew the most about me, and who loved me anyway. At 10:34 P.M. I had been a distraught but still happily married mother of two. Sixty seconds later my two sons were fatherless and I was a widow.

I was not allowed to be with Phil right after he died; the hospital staff had to clean him up after their failed lifesaving attempts. When I was finally permitted back into the room, they had wrapped his body in plastic up to his shoulders and put a blanket over him. And then it occurred to me, I wanted his wedding band. I had to have it. Right then. I didn't want to wait. I called the nurse and she sliced the plastic open; I lifted his left hand out and pulled the ring off his long, lifeless finger. I placed his ring behind my own wedding band on my left finger, my smaller band keeping his from falling off. I was preserving our union, keeping him with me, the only way I could think of.

Alone in Phil's parents' house six months after he died, I found myself crying over the loss of all the things I would never feel again: Phil's hand on my lower back, his weight on top of me, my arm wrapped around his waist, my lips on the nape of his neck, my toe running down the length of his leg as I sidled up next to him in bed. I cried because I finally felt Phil's physical absence, and I couldn't stop crying because what I had left didn't feel like enough. I couldn't imagine living my life, much less one more second, without his touch. It occurred to me then that I hadn't been embraced or held by anyone since Phil died. I missed human contact terribly.

Eight months after Phil died, I started playing ring gymnastics, moving the wedding rings into different configurations on my fingers. I took my own band off and moved Phil's to the middle finger of my right hand. Wearing my wedding ring no longer felt "right," it felt like I was faking, trying to be something I wasn't: married. Soon after, Phil's ring began to feel uncomfortable, and I decided I needed to take this small weight off my fingers. Finally, one day, with little fanfare, I removed Phil's wedding band.

As more months passed, I slipped out of shock and I started to feel again. I needed intimacy, I needed human contact. I needed to feel like more than a professional and widowed mother of two small children. I tentatively researched a couple of online dating websites. With some cajoling from my friend Mare, who was newly separated, and who joined me on this new adventure, I started first with a no cost site. A couple of weeks later, I summoned my courage and posted a full profile and pictures. It was hard and I felt vulnerable, but it was tolerable because I had a partner in crime and we tried not to take it too seriously. Mare and I would laugh like 8th grade schoolgirls at the profiles we saw, the emails we received, the sheer absurdity of it all as we shopped for intimacy. And then one day, I the daily email from one of the dating sites included the profiles of a number of eligible bachelors.

> "Wearing my wedding ring no longer felt 'right', it felt like I was faking, trying to be something I wasn't: married."

I clicked on one that I thought was cute, and I read his demographics: 45, father of two, a Virgo and recent widower. I wrote an email: "I think we might have some things in common." I received an email back a few days later, "I think we do—Tom."

"What do you want to do," he asked slyly as we leaned against the wall, the rain falling around us. I paused and then said, truthfully, "What I really want is for you to come to my apartment so that we can make out on my couch, and then I want you to leave before morning." He replied, "Okay, as long as we can be naked." I agreed. We hopped in a cab and headed north, his hands caressing my thigh in a familiar way.

At 2:00 A.M. I did the walk of shame past my doorman. I introduced Tom as my "friend" to the new babysitter and hurried her out the door; my need to see where the kissing, touching and flirtation would go was greater than any concerns about what people would think.

We made our way to my bedroom, where we ended my 1 year and 10 months of celibacy, and after I shooed Tom out my front door at 4:00 A.M., I collapsed into bed and, despite all of the thoughts swirling in my mind, I fell asleep in minutes.

To my surprise, when I awoke the next morning, I felt fine. Tired, but fine. The first text came while I slept. He'd had to wait for over an hour at Penn Station for a train back to Long Island but it had been more than worth it. His second text came while I was telling my shocked and amused friend Dee what I had been up to the night before while my son had a sleepover at her place. His text read, "Why is it that I can't stop thinking about you." I passed my fingers over an emerging beard burn on my chin. A knowing smirk broadened into a self-satisfied smile, and I thought, *I just had sex with someone 1 year and 10 months after the death of my husband of 14 years.*

My relationship with Tom, nice as he was, was short lived. But, the brevity of our time together belies its import. That first "morning after," was not unlike what I imagine a victim of a car crash experiences. I checked to make sure everything was okay and working—arms (check), legs (check), breathing (check), mind (check)—yes, I was alive. I just had sex with someone other than my husband whom I had been with for so very long. And I was okay. No, better than okay, I was good.

I had survived the car crash. I was alive. Again.

Elissa L. Perry is the mother of two boys, ages five and seven. A college professor, she teaches and conducts research on topics related to workplace discrimination. She lives with her children on the Upper West Side of Manhattan.

Unintended Consequences

Jane Rowan

I didn't intend to pursue the arts. I didn't intend to make a grab at an early retirement offer and leave teaching, a job that I loved. I certainly didn't intend to find out about childhood incest.

These days I spend my mornings painting abstract canvases or writing. Those days, I got up hurriedly, checked my to-do lists, grabbed my briefcase already loaded with student papers and lecture notes, and headed off to the office. I would not have moved from there to here without the raging crisis that began with an unexpected memory.

On a humid early August morning, I was waking slowly when a feeling emerged from a dim corner of my mind. I sat up in bed and began scribbling in my journal, remembering when I was three or four and, and perched on the toilet, I hurt between my legs. I felt the sting when I peed. Fear sank its claws into my stomach. I wondered what had happened and whether someone had molested me. I had no memory of what had caused the hurt. Surely it couldn't have been my father, I thought, as my stomach clenched.

That was Revelation Day, the day that started me on a long journey into my past. How did it happen that a 52 year-old woman suddenly woke up to the possibility of long-ago abuse? What had kept the issues at bay so long? How could the past now grab me by the throat?

At that point I had been divorced for ten years, after a long marriage. I had a college-age son, several good friends, and stable family ties. My father had died a year previously at the age of eighty-three, after a long battle with Parkinson's disease. My elderly mother lived alone about two hours away from my home. I taught organic chemistry at a liberal arts college and was successful in my work. I loved the give-and-take of classroom teaching as well as the opportunity to guide individual students' lives. I devised exercises to induce students to work collaboratively and learn from one another in class, feeling the satisfaction of stepping aside while they shone. I became a teacher's teacher, giving workshops to faculty at other colleges and universities. At this time of my life, my expertise in teaching methods was being recognized.

I was a scientist. Evidence was my bread and butter. Even though I'd moved on from laboratory research to administration, there was nothing I liked better than a juicy set of numbers. Scientific arguments could be fierce and competitive, but they were based on demonstrable facts. I didn't yet realize there was knowledge more important than facts.

After the memory came, I dug out old pictures. I gazed at the girl in the black-and-white photographs, the one in the Girl Scout uniform, with the long braids, the first-grader in the school picture wearing the cotton dress with puffy sleeves, looking solemn—*could* she have been molested, abused? It was true that I didn't smile in the pictures, but surely what I remembered was a normal childhood. I veered back and forth. Believing that something happened, I felt guilty and intensely disloyal for accusing my family of such a thing. Not believing, I felt crazy, as if I'd explode.

Fortunately, I was seeing a therapist whom I trusted. In her quiet office, my therapist listened to my incoherent story, my false starts on sentences, the things blurted out. "I remembered this time… I know I was three or four because we only lived in that house for a short while. I'm sitting on the toilet and it hurts when I pee. It stings. My mother says that I slipped on the bathtub over there and hurt myself on the rim, but that isn't true. *It's not!*" My shoulders and stomach were tight as I struggled to speak. "After I was finished going to the bathroom, my mother would wash me with boric acid to take away the sting. Somehow I remember that's what it was called, 'boric acid.'" I remembered the cool sensation of the washcloth between my legs. "But I don't remember anybody doing anything to me," I wailed, feeling scared and dizzy with uncertainty.

"Do you have any sense who it might have been?" the therapist asked.

"No, not really. But it feels like it had to be my father. But I don't know! It's all really vague except that memory about peeing. How do I know if it's real?"

"People don't make these things up for fun," she said.

I took a deep breath and sighed. "I feel so sad. Why am I sad? I just want to cry and cry."

"It's all right to cry."

And I did. Even though I didn't yet believe my memory, I began mourning for the relationships I thought I had, the ones I wanted and needed, the safe mother and father. I mourned for the picture of a family that I had carried all this time, a normal-enough family to raise a normal-enough person.

My family was both eccentric and loving. In many ways my parents were wonderful. My father was an independent consulting engineer who ran his business from the basement of our house. All I had to do was open my bedroom door and walk down the stairs, and there was his desk. In the other downstairs rooms, his oddball employees worked and chatted. He was a fervent Old Leftist who believed in equality and justice. Father taught me many technical skills and made me feel smart.

My mother ran the practical side of the business and kept Father from making crazy investments. When he was angry and temperamental, she seethed but stayed out of the way. She was talented in mathematics and writing, but she was overshadowed by his moods and impulses. Perhaps because of her difficult childhood, with her father dying of Lou Gehrig's disease and a cold, hard-working mother, she avoided emotions and kept busy. She used denial as her shield and sword, but at the same time, I knew there was a part of her that desired intimacy. Caught between the two of them, I became a good, dependable girl.

After the first memory came, I wrestled for a year with doubt about whether anything at all had happened to me as a child. Then, just as I was involved in two conferences and writing a major grant, another came. At least you might call it memory—I had a body-sensation of my mouth being stuffed full, gagging and nausea. If I'd been awash before, now I was in spin cycle. Unwanted, uncontrollable body-memories flooded me at inconvenient times. They convinced me that something had indeed happened to me.

The million-dollar grant I'd written came through, bringing new opportunities and new pressure. One day I was in my office typing at the computer when a colleague came to the doorway. I swiveled my chair to face him. "There's this great opportunity for student research," he said. "We are eager to get going on it. Can't you just release some funds now, and I'll apply for something later?" I knew that he was sincere and an excellent teacher who attracted students into research, but his tone of expecting to get his own way triggered a wave of fear.

"The committee," I said, "You need to apply through the regular procedure."

"But we want to start in two weeks. I don't see why you can't..." He came closer, still talking.

I stood up, not knowing quite why, but now I see, not wanting to be sitting with my face just below his belt buckle. "The committee. It's not my decision." *That's exactly why I set it up this way*, I thought through the murk of emotions. *So it's not a matter of your pressuring me to get what you assume you deserve to have.*

When he left, I sat back down heavily, my mouth feeling stuffed full and my stomach twisting. *Breathe*, I thought. *Breathe. Remember it's not the same now. It's not like that. I have the power now, not him.*

It took me a while to understand that these flashbacks were just as real as those of a war veteran. The word "flashback" fooled me into thinking of scenes where "it all comes back," as in the movies. But my therapist kept telling me, "Most people don't ever get complete pictures, just bits and pieces." I also read articles about Post-Traumatic Stress Disorder which showed that traumatic memory is often fragmented. For a veteran it might be the instinctive dive under the table in response to a loud noise. For an abuse survivor, it can be the pressure in the mouth, nausea, an ache in low in the belly, or fear in situations that seem ordinary but are obscurely threatening.

I didn't intend to spend several years immersed in the waters of my psyche, but my emotions left me no choice. My lifelines were my therapist, my friends, and my creative outlets. My therapist taught me to listen to the voice of the little girl inside me who had been molested and who felt intensely abandoned by both parents. I set aside time to listen to this inner child daily.

Currents of ancient emotions swept through me. In therapy and in my daily life, I crawled through thickets of mistrust and bogs of shame. I was enraged at people who trampled my boundaries. Fogs of dissociation blurred the contours of my world. And yet I functioned well at work and kept up friendships. Slowly, my focus shifted away from the misery and need of the child inside me. As I began to trust my therapist's love and acceptance, I gained a sense of being a sturdy, worthy person who had already survived the worst.

I wouldn't have called it creativity at first. I simply needed to write in my journal every day, keeping track of my feelings as they swirled. I'd sit at the kitchen table and let my pen race, uncensored. But words were limiting, too. When I was abused at age three to six, I didn't have words for what happened. When I had tried to tell my mother, she responded with fear, impatience, and, "Forget it—that's all you can do." I didn't get a chance to articulate what had happened or to experience support. Fifty years later I needed to involve the wordless, unscientific parts of my mind in the work of recovery.

I took up pastels and scribbled dark, angry pages full of red and black. Meanwhile my mother was aging and needed my help and attention. I drove the eighty miles each month to help with household work and then to help her remain independent as she grew blind from macular degeneration. We shopped for gadgets; I labeled appliances and thermostats with large numbers. Her dependence on me sharpened the burn of feeling that she'd abandoned me and turned a blind eye to my father's abuse.

Mother was diagnosed with colon cancer. She chose not to have surgery. My sister and I supported her in the decision. In the few months she had left, would I confront her about the abuse? Talking with my therapist, I saw that it was unlikely I'd gain a sudden breakthrough of intimacy and forgiveness with Mother. I decided not to speak.

Through all this I continued with the repetitive, frightening work of coming to terms with the abuse and with my family. I never quite understood why my mother was so cowed by life and so depressed, because she refused to talk about the past. She regularly turned away from emotional topics, clearing her throat and asking, "So, what are we having for dinner?" She did the best she could, and I always knew she loved me, although her range of expression was limited.

The question of my father was even thornier. He loved me, no doubt at all. As a socialist and thinker, he was capable of empathy for the downtrodden. How could he have ignored my terror? Perhaps he'd been abused as a child—certainly his relationship to his mother was intense and difficult. Time and again, my therapist sighed and said, "Some things are just not explainable." I can't say I've forgiven him, because I still believe there's no excusing his behavior. But I have come to feel my love for him as well as his for me. I wouldn't say he did the best he could, as Mother did, but his quirky personality, his intense interests, and his affection have traveled with me all my life.

Over those years of recovery, as I sat at my kitchen table after work and covered acres of paper with my slanting, illegible scrawl, I let words emerge like creatures from the chaos of my subconscious. I learned to listen to the ones that spoke back to me, mirroring the turmoil.

The year my mother died, I joined a writing group. My flooding grief mixed with anger at her limited, timid life and poured into poems. About six months after her death I had the inspiration to write a memoir about my healing process. The project took me by the throat and would not let go. When my college offered an early retirement package, I accepted instantly. Obviously, I would have retired at some point and might have stayed partly engaged in my profession. But I left early, with less money, to go towards a creative, more fulfilling life.

> "I sat back down heavily. Breathe, I thought. Breathe. Remember it's not the same now. I have the power now, not him."

Art was a further stretch. It had been a forbidden area. When I was a kid, I was good at everything *except* art. Seeing my attempts at drawing, my mother laughed and said, "Well, you're no artist," and it stuck. In the anger and confusion that surged in me, I began scribbling. It was by necessity uncensored. When no words could touch the desolation and incredulous sting of betrayal, I would fist a black crayon and transfer its soul onto the page, adding jagged red, brown, purple slashes. I ground the colors onto the page until I felt a satisfaction of release inside—*That's it. That is really the way it feels.* Art was a place beyond judgment. Over and over, I assured myself, *This is just for me, not for anyone to judge.* When my therapist said, "This is really expressive—I hope someone else is seeing it," I brushed her comments aside.

But art-as-therapy gave birth to art-as-play. Now as I survey a canvas in progress, of course the critical voices hover nearby and whisper, *You have no idea what you are doing. Quit that. You never could draw. What makes you think you can do this?* My pulse quickens, but then I talk myself through it.

How can I articulate the newness of this way of living, of being free to express my innermost feelings? As I express my emotions through art, I can feel the earthquake sensation of reinventing my world. It's not that my life turned perfect. I'd love to say that I'm an artist completely free in my creation and in my sharing with the world. I'd love to envision this wild-haired, wild-eyed woman with a girl-spirit ready for anything, joyous every day. What I've got, however, is a woman who has turned from a scientist into an artist. A woman who has dared to venture into her inner world The strong emotions that flowed through me in the work of recovering from abuse were like a fire-hose sweeping aside old obstacles and criticisms, making space for new ways of being.

I am still my mother's daughter—the persistence and discipline, the stubbornness. I am still my father's daughter—the quest for something more, dashing off on new projects, the inventiveness. But I am my own daughter as well, the beloved creative child.

———————————

Jane Rowan, Ph.D. is a retired college teacher who has published numerous articles and poems. She is the author of a self-help booklet, *Caring for the Child Within*. She has written a memoir, *Beyond Memory: My Journey of Healing from Incest*.

Treatment

Susannah Risley

A few years ago, in a treatment center in Florida, a therapist advised me to try to get Social Security insurance benefits when I returned home to Massachusetts. This was right after they told me in a progress meeting that I was mentally ill, probably bipolar. I clutched the seat of the orange plastic chair and started to sob. The people in the little circle that surrounded me looked shocked. Perhaps they thought learning I could get paid for my problems would be a kind of reward, so I really shouldn't take it so hard. Like if you're a double Gemini you get to be highly creative, though you pay for it in the stability department.

A treatment center in Florida. It sounds similar to a dude ranch in Wyoming, though it would be sun and tropical waters that restored you to your senses instead of cowboys and huge starry nights. But this particular hospital was in an inland suburb. It was August, and the blacktop of the parking lot tended to get mushy in the early afternoon. We were mostly women, mining the soil beneath various addictions for roots, decay, and new seeds. It was a hopeful place, but for me the candlelight flickered when they told me I was mentally ill. Here's why:

Most of my life had been an effort to fit in and hide the fact that I wasn't an earthling. I thought other people had some form of dance lessons marked out at birth on their personal floors: put your left foot here, right foot there, add the music and voila, a dance. I always seemed to be stuck at the level of placing—what was it now, the *left* foot—onto the diagram and then trying to figure out which was my right foot and how to get it onto the next painted foot. Never mind the music. I'd picture myself lurching along, in a room filled with dancing couples flowing all around me, their eyes gazing into each other's while *my* eyes were glued to my oxfords, trying to will the next step.

Not that I saw myself as a victim. You might think being told I was mentally ill would have been a relief. I could blame all that discomfort on body chemistry or sailing on a vast, empty, inner sea. Instead I felt like a stern dance teacher with over-bleached hair and a wooden pointer had nailed me. At the hospital they kept asking me what I wanted when I got all emotionally unhinged, which was often. After all, I figured it *was* a mental hospital, wasn't it a place to forget about etiquette and reason? Not that I could really control my responses. Laughing quickly became hysteria and shifted into weeping, as if I had an inner automatic transmission that just kept shifting through the emotional gears. I guess that made some of the other patients and the staff wary about telling jokes at the dinner table. It made me feel wary also. I was used to being aloof.

What did I want? That wasn't a question I'd thought much about during my survival scramble. I mulled it over in my room at night until I was able to articulate a vague, tribal instinct, more of a body wish than a thought. It was simple: I wanted to be among people, nothing more. So patients were asked and it was agreed that I could come into their rooms at times and sit on the extra standard beige chair and be in their company while they read or knitted or watched television. I wanted to be in the presence of another person without any demands made on me to be smart or pretty or emotionally correct. The way Eskimos visit, often without saying a word.

I started to calm down after a few weeks of being in other people's orbits and attending the recovery meetings, therapy and daily exercise class. The Gestalt psychiatrist decided maybe I wasn't crazy after all, just a person with a lot of stored-up energy. Even without their opinions, I knew I didn't want to try to get on disability for mental illness or anything else. I would end up in some dreary, tiny apartment with faded wallpaper, really buying into being mentally ill so that I could receive my check every month. The days would pass like those of Virginia Woolf during a down time, but without the pleasure of interesting visitors. I'd be glued to myself like a television set.

They must have had another staff meeting at the treatment center. Their next suggestion was that I try for Social Security for simply emotional and physical exhaustion. I'd somehow managed to spend most of my life fairly isolated from people, on the move and bouncing through addictions like a marble in a pinball machine. I tended towards jobs where I could be invisible; I had the resume of a secret agent. The romantic relationships I'd had seemed plotted with the intensity of a Russian novel. Once, upon waking up with a man with long black hair and a "Born to Run" T-shirt, I suspected that during blackouts I might have answered personal ads in prison magazines.

I decided not to try for Social Security and not to be mentally ill. The more they talked to me about it at the hospital the more resolved I became. I was fed up with being the designated crazy, a role I'd assumed in my family early on. It wasn't like I was having radio waves from Saturn beamed into my glass's frames when I went grocery shopping. I was broken hearted, jammed up, fogged in, but not crazy. I could tell the difference. I needed to stop drinking and doping myself; I needed to tell the truth about my busted heart so that I could begin to feel it beating again. I needed to believe I could trust who I was.

I thought of Norman Cousin's famous cure for a mysterious, would-be fatal disease. He checked out of the hospital and into a hotel room where he watched Marx Brothers movies and other comedies and surrounded himself with cheerful people. I could do something similar. I could watch slice-of life movies about connections between people. I could watch "Thelma and Louise" about a hundred times, pressing the "rewind" button just before they drove off the cliff. I'd still have to get out the door and into the world, probably the hardest part. Was it really safe out there without a few dozen crutches?

It was a good thing I decided not to be crazy. It would have been a strain to handle the situation when I returned home. I discovered that the man who was to sublet my apartment for two months, a recovering heroin addict I'd met just once through a friend in AA, had hit the streets instead. Luckily my neighbor wouldn't give him the key when he showed up to collect it; he was acting too weird. So I was down two months' rent, which equaled being flat broke, but at least I still had my type-writer. There wasn't too much else he could have taken. As part of my after-care program, I'd promised to get furniture as a commitment to a more permanent lifestyle.

> "I'd dash from scrubbing a floor to a teaching stint with barely enough time to wipe off the sweat. I cried. I laughed. I got stronger."

I felt like a newly hatched bird as I sat on the carpeted floor in my living room. I felt grief because I'd sort of forgotten to have a life, with some gratitude creeping in because I wasn't caught in the foggy marsh of denial any longer. I took out the "Feelings Finder" they'd given me in rehab, a few pages of rows of cartoon faces expressing one emotion or another. At first, in the hospital, the sad or mad faces were all I could identify with, but now I was starting to get into more subtle shadings. Let's see, where *was* that face called Terror? The phone rang.

It was the business office of the hospital in Florida. Due to an insurance problem at the private school where I'd worked nights, I was now expected to pay the whole bill for treatment. The hospital wanted me to send them thousands of dollars immediately. The billing office did not seem to care if I could identify all the feelings I was having at that moment. They did not ask me to find the appropriate face on the Feeling Finder. It was as if they couldn't have cared less if I were mentally ill or if they were pushing me over the edge.

I put down the phone and started to feel faint. I checked my wallet to see if I had enough money to cover a few bottles of Nyquil, just in case. This one day at a time thing looked a little brutal. I had enough cash to put me in a coma for two or three days, *surely* enough time for things to straighten themselves out.

I ran downstairs and unlocked my car, which had been parked for two months. It started, but once I got on the street the front wheel began to scream like a woman in labor. People on the sidewalk were looking, and I had a sudden urge to run them over. After a few blocks I pulled over and parked, got out and slammed the door. I kicked the tire and swore loud enough to offend all those nosy, self-righteous passersby who probably had their rent all paid and someone to talk to if a hospital called asking them to go into debt for life. Plus they probably weren't as *sensitive* as I was, or manic-depressive, and they didn't have to look on some stupid piece of paper to figure out they were pissed.

And neither did I. I walked to an AA meeting in a local church basement. People were sitting on folding chairs at long wooden tables. There were several empty seats. I sat down feeling like I'd been caught naked in public. ("Vulnerable," was my guess that the Feelings Finder would call it.) A speaker stood at a podium and talked about holding up a bank during a blackout, then spending years in prison for a crime he never remembered committing. He made jokes about it and people laughed. He talked about how the whole thing taught him a lot about humility and powerlessness. He talked about shedding the cocoon of self-pity along with the alcohol and the feeling of being special and entirely alone. I started to calm down a little, but at the end of the meeting when everyone held hands and said the Serenity Prayer, I was so moved I started to cry. I left quickly, unsure if the laughing would kick in next. Instead of getting the Nyquil, I went home and threw pillows around until I was worn out and peaceful: a cheap, natural high.

I started calling people I knew vaguely and asked for advice about the insurance situation. I found out about the Insurance Commissioner, how to write to him and also about the Labor Board. It turned out they'd been watching the school where I worked, waiting for someone to come in with a substantial complaint so they could go in and look at the school's books. I filled out forms. I talked with lawyers at the Labor Board. I answered ads to do cleaning in places close enough to walk. Eventually I fixed my car. I learned to sit through an AA meeting with my mind a bit quieter and see that I was among friends.

I took on more house cleaning jobs. I also started teaching a writing group at the local Women's Center. I was awed by many of the stories that were read by group members, though I started to notice a pattern: just when the story reached a point where anger or fear or pain had to be expressed, the writer often veered off, often settling for depression instead. This made me anxious; it was just a little too close to home. I started to bring the Feelings Finder to class."Okay," I'd ask, "instead of being depressed, she *really* feels…" and we'd look at the faces snarling with rage, heavy with grief, a timid face, a sad one, and we'd try out different possible endings. Different ways of seeing our feelings.

Later, I volunteered to work with kids in a reform school. I expanded the cleaning jobs because they paid so well, and I kept advertising for new writing instruction jobs. Sometimes I'd dash from scrubbing a floor to a teaching stint with barely enough time to wipe off the sweat. I cried. I laughed. I got stronger. I listened to Aretha Franklin tapes on my Walkman as I vacuumed and started thinking of her as a higher power, one that would do until I figured out a more complex spirituality.

One of the people who answered my ad was a psychoanalyst at a famous Berkshire mental institution. His wife, an English professor, claimed his articles had been rejected because his writing style was too passive. He'd withered beneath the judgment as if that critical dancing teacher with the bleached hair I knew so intimately had made it. For two hours a week, for six months, for a handsome fee, it was now one of my jobs to sit in a leather chair in his elegant office while he read his stories to me and sunlight inched its way across the oriental carpet—stories usually about the doctor's father, a man who could not be pleased. I'd make suggestions to face the emotional issues that were blocking his expression, and to go through it. I never told the doctor that before and after our meetings I cleaned houses.

At times, the doctor would just start talking to me about his father. I'd sit in the matching leather chair and listen attentively. Despite the movie-set surroundings, the psychoanalyst was just another person telling his tale. Haven't we all lived the same life, after all? My job then was to listen and not say a word; the way Eskimos visit, with an open heart and a quiet mind.

Susannah Risley has published fiction and essays in *Redbook, Mademoiselle* and *Poets & Writers* magazines. She is the recipient of a James Michener Award from the University of Iowa Writers' Workshop and held a Fellowship at the MacDowell Colony. She has taught many writing workshops in libraries, schools, prisons, senior centers and homeless shelters throughout New York State.

Smashed Open

Erin Harvey

It is the first cool night in Virginia, with a hint of fall in the air. I have always hated winter, but today I'm enjoying the fresh air and the ability to get a deep breath. I grew up in Mississippi, where you don't get a deep breath until December and only if you're lucky. My dad still takes the phone on my rare call home and that's all he wants to talk about: the weather. "Man, it sure was hot today. What's it been like up there with the Yankees?"

Growing up, I always thought my dad "got me." That we were both level-headed communicators except for those times when he would go into one of his moods, as my mother called them. A true extrovert just like me, to all of my friends he was this goofy, joke-telling sort of guy, except for these moods of his. The summer before 9th grade we started a business together cutting grass, and I witnessed these moods first hand when the lawn mower wouldn't crank. This was the same summer that I got boobs and starting wondering why I couldn't beat my best friend in the 800 yard race anymore. Some other "loose" girls (as my dad called them when he drove through the Pizza Hut parking lot to show my sister and me what loose meant) would have jumped at the chance for boobs and a butt, but I was oblivious. I just wanted to know why I was gaining weight and what I had to do to stop it.

Unfortunately, my growing boobs were uncomfortable for all of us, especially my white collar southern Baptist preacher father and my

Erin Harvey

appearance-aware mother. However, my older sister, four years my sen-ior, who hid cookies under her bed to spite my mother, couldn't get enough of it. She relished the fact that she was not the only one who couldn't eat everything in sight and get away with it. The same sister who came home drunk at fifteen after driving twenty miles from her summer lifeguard job. The same sister I saw my father slap in the face that night, and preach about immorality the next day at Sunday School. The same sister who caused my father to come get me, drag me upstairs and show me her drunken face to teach me a lesson of what a drunk looked like. I didn't sleep upstairs for a week until my parents sat me down and told me that I was going to have to see the doctor if I didn't start sleeping in my own bed again. I was eleven.

No wonder I was concerned about keeping everyone in the house happy and calm. No wonder I could never be silly and carefree. No wonder I was codependent. You probably don't understand what being a codependent person means unless you've had the great pleasure of meeting one of us. We are the ones who cannot say no to anything. and we keep everyone "happy." Without us, there would be no non-profits or volunteer groups. We care. And often, we care way too much.

Looking back, it seems obvious that I would fall for an alcoholic. That he would be the first one that I told I loved. It is now obvious that I was continuing behaviors that I had learned as a child. But I didn't see it. I just saw this hot medical student who was the smartest, cutest person I had ever met. Someone who told me he loved me for the first time while making love. Someone who spent the night with me every night since that first time we went home together. Someone who needed me. Of course I should have seen the signs. The New Year's Eve in New York when I had to be the responsible one with directions, even though he went to undergraduate school at New York's Cooper Union, an engineering school for the geniuses. Or the birthday I spent alone because he had been drunk for four days straight and had forgotten it.

Everyone around me should have told me what they saw, but they didn't, and it wouldn't have made a difference. I was in love. I was in love for the first time and my eyes were closed. I couldn't see it. I couldn't see the times he put me down and made me feel ashamed because I wasn't as smart as he and his family. I couldn't see the days going by of him not calling and me wondering what I did wrong. I couldn't see that each of these acts was causing me to lose myself, to forget my own needs, to put my future in someone else's hands. Of course there were break-ups and threats of leaving him. But I could never stand up to his apologies. Apologies filled with tears and promises.

I moved to D.C. with him. He had matched at Georgetown in a program that accepts only four interns a year. How proud we felt when we packed only what we could fit in my car and drove away cursing Mississippi for being so closed-minded and suffocating. How excited we felt when we cooked dinner together for the first time in our apartment. Oh, the future looked so bright!

I never would have guessed that within four months I would be in the back seat of a white BMW, listening to Dolly Parton while two gay dudes drove us to rehab. Of course, he was the only one being admitted. This was two weeks after I had gotten home from work one afternoon and he wouldn't wake up. After I sat counting the pills and calling the psychiatrist asking what to do. After I ran around D.C. begging a cabdriver to take us all the way out to Bethesda to the hospital because every one of the emergency rooms in the District was affiliated with Georgetown. That night I watched as he was checked into the psych ward.

Fortunately, six months later, after rehab and a halfway house, he was sober. The day I picked him up, we made love in his halfway house. I got a job in Charlottesville, Virginia and we fled the city and all of its horrible memories. Hope once again! We had made it. Of course he would finally say thank you for saving my life and propose to me. Of course he would finally get a real job and stop yelling at me about money. But he didn't. Instead, one month later, after a sleepless night of fighting, he confessed to me that he "never wanted to get married in my parents freaking backyard."

"What? After all I have done for you! After all that I have sacrificed! It still isn't enough for you to give up your selfishness and love me?" No. It wasn't. After two months of living together again, our hopes had died. We broke up.

Here I was in a new place with a new job and scared to death. I decided it was finally time to ask for help. I needed my mother. I needed someone to make me chicken 'n' dumplings and help me find a place to live. I needed a hug. She never came. She said she couldn't find a straight flight into Charlottesville and just couldn't handle the stress of changing planes. I had never felt so alone. Thankfully, my friend Laura called from the Charlottesville airport that Saturday to ask if I could pick her up. What are friends for? To create the family you need to get through this horrible life.

And that is exactly what I did. Soon after the breakup, I started seeing a therapist who helped me change my life. I took it by the horns. The only thing I knew to do was to go at it full force. To open my eyes to this mess of a life that I had created and try to get better. I learned to stop feeling sorry for myself while realizing that I was this way because of my family history, and that I was the only one who was going to change my life. I found myself sitting in support groups that were supposed to help those of us who loved alcoholics and thinking, "Why doesn't she just leave him? She has no idea how good her life could be!"

> "I took it by the horns. The only thing I knew to do was to go at it full force. To open my eyes to this mess of a life that I had created and try to get better."

I stopped going to the meetings. I started reading every self-help book I could get my hands on. I made friends. I got drunk. I danced. I met boys. I had sex! I didn't agree to anything I didn't want to do. I stood up for myself. I yelled at my neighbors. I told my boss what I really thought, and I didn't get fired. For the first time in my life, I could finally breathe. Of course it wasn't easy, and still there are times when I wake up from a dream so terrible that it makes me want to build a fort under the sheets and stay there. But I wouldn't change anything. I never understood how people could go through such tragedies and make statements like that, but now I do. I was miserable even before falling in love with this alcoholic and never even knew it. Now I wouldn't change a thing about my life because it led to the lessons I've learned and the lessons that I am still learning.

I'm not sure if time heals everything. Maybe time and fighting do, digging in the dirt to get a breath, the one that will get you through to the next minute. If you are lucky, the next hour. Sometimes you see the sun and that spurs you on until the next day, even. And then one day you look around and you see green, not brown. You smell clean air, not earthy mud. You can stand on the ground firmly, not cling to the edge of the cliff for your life. You can stretch out, open your arms wide to the blue sky and before you know it, you've made it.

It was a year this past July that we broke up. I survived the holidays and anniversary dates and even a meeting with the Ex. I also found a great job and got the heck out of Charlottesville. The overall experience caused me to look to what I really need to survive. No, not just to survive, but to be happy. Does true happiness exist? I have no idea. But what I do know is that happy moments exist and I deserve to have more of them.

————————

Originally from Mississippi, Erin Harvey lives in Virginia, where she works as an exercise physiologist.

Patching Together a Life

Glynis Scrivens

This morning I got an email from a well known English magazine writer asking me how I went from being virtually disabled from illness to being so productive. The answer could be in a scrap of fabric. Well, make that 180 of them.

When I was 32, I faced death from a devastating illness. I lay there experiencing the fading of the light, wondering what would await me on the other side. I survived my narrow brush with the End, but having my life collapse into myriad pieces was devastating. I looked at the ruins that represented my identity: friendships, memories, skills, work, family, achievements. And I wondered how I'd ever glue it all back together. Due to my illness, I knew that from then on, any life worth living would only be the result of a lot of hard work. Would I have the energy? Was there any glue left?

But time passed, however slowly, and eventually a realization dawned on me. The crisis that had brought me to this point had an unexpected bonus—it presented me with new opportunity. In spite of the difficulties my illness would continue to cause, I began to feel a dizzying sense of freedom: the freedom to transform myself. To create the person I wanted to be.

Armed with this inspiration, I set about reshaping my life. The first decision was the hardest. I needed to find a way in which I could make a valuable contribution, within the physical confines imposed by my

Glynis Scrivens

illness. As my symptoms fluctuated, I needed work that could accommodate my absence during relapses, and also that could expand during a period of improved health.

By coincidence, my patchwork quilt had also come to a crossroads. I'd made it while my father and my husband made our bed, years ago. It had spent nine summers and nine winters on active duty, its wear and tear accelerating once young children wrestled on it and sticky fingers explored the colorful patches. Like me, it looked ready for the scrap heap.

One day my husband gently hand-washed it and hung it out on the line to dry. I looked out the kitchen window and saw it with all its imperfections highlighted by the afternoon sun. There were dangling pieces where the quilt had been torn. Parts of it were so threadbare it was almost transparent.

Like my body, it would need a lot of work to make it usable again, and I just couldn't bring myself to throw it out. But making another patchwork quilt was out of the question because I had no energy. That left mending, a very daunting prospect. How would I replace 180 patchwork squares? The answer was simple: one at a time. As I am a natural hoarder, there was no shortage of patches. So when I was well enough, I began to sew one patch onto the quilt each afternoon. And because I could only manage one new square each day, I thought carefully about my choice—in a way I hadn't done the first time around, when I'd been in perfect health and only thought of the quilt as functional. This time I found scraps of fabric that held meaning for me, so that seeing them in my quilt would make me feel good.

> "In spite of the difficulties my illness would cause, I began to feel a dizzying sense of freedom: the freedom to transform myself. To create the person I wanted to be."

As the number of new pieces grew, so did my positive feelings about my new life. The quilt and I were both being visibly repaired in subtle ways. And the new patches brightened up my whole bedroom, symbolizing fresh hopes and dreams—while incorporating happy memories from the past.

There were all kinds of squares—the pink floral I'd used to brighten a patchwork dress I'd sewn for my daughter and the blue Hawaiian print I'd used to make beach shorts for my son. There were bright floral remnants from the scrunchies I'd made to hold my other daughter's ponytails and the cream fabric from my first attempt at smocking a dress for my baby. These pieces represented the richness of my life and reminded me of happier days.

Then my quilt took on an extra dimension. Once my supply of scraps began to dwindle, I asked my sister for her remnants. These too held special memories. Then my favorite aunt embroidered a bunch of cherries for me, so I sewed on a tiny border and added it to the quilt. My mother unearthed a scrap from a dress I could remember my grandmother sewing on her old treadle machine. And when my mother visited my brother in England, she brought me home a piece they'd chosen together especially for the quilt. Over the course of a year, the quilt went from being a shabby, functional piece to a cheerful amalgamation of family treasures and memories. So did I.

Today my life is like this quilt—full of carefully chosen pieces. With limited energy and health, I've had to let go of the negatives I used to cling to in the past and hold fast to the positive. But I've done it. I've gone beyond the quilt to a busy career I can handle while managing my energy: writing. So when that writer emailed me this morning and asked, "How do you do it?" I thought of the quilt. I would have told her about everything down to the last square, until I realized I have too much work to do. So I boiled it down to 4 simple steps:

1. Have your life collapse around you.

2. Think about it long and hard.

3. Somewhere in that swirl of emotion, find the positive.

4. Cling to the meaningful and release the rest.

It worked for me.

Glynis Scrivens lives in Brisbane, with her husband, three children, and a menagerie of pets. She writes fiction for women's magazines and is a regular contributor to *Writers' Forum* magazine.

PART TWO

Finding My Calling

Escape

Christina Heyniger

On my first big whitewater river trip in the Grand Canyon, the thrumming approach of the rapids, combined with the powerful pounding of the blood in my temples, was loud enough to drown out everything, including coherent thought. When you see a big wave in the river ahead, even after you've been down a few rivers and know what to expect, you feel scared. The only thing calming for me on that trip was focusing on the guide's voice. I was just one of 12 other guests on a commercial river trip in the Grand Canyon, but that trip, and my response to it, set in motion a chain of events that baffles me—and a lot of my friends and family—to this day.

When I returned to my office in Washington, D.C., the joy and excitement of my Grand Canyon adventure seemed like a delusional dream. *Had I ever even been there?* Sitting in my 11th floor office, I returned to the routines of my life as unceremoniously as if the trip had never happened. My days went like this:

6:00–6:30 A.M.—Wake up, get dressed to go to the gym.

6:30–6:40—Drive to the gym.

6:45—Put work clothes in locker.

7:00–8:00—Exercise.

8:30—Shower and get dressed for work.

Christina Heyniger

8:30–9:15—Drive to work.

9:15–11:00—Morning segment. Drink water.

11:00–11:10—Go down to the lobby and look around, come back up, use the restroom.

11:10–12:30—Mid-morning segment. Eat an apple/banana/granola bar.

12:30–1:15 P.M.—Lunch

1:15–3:00—Early afternoon segment. Drink tea/water.

3:00–3:10—Go down to the lobby and look around, come back up, use the restroom.

3:10–5:00 — Late afternoon segment. Eat apple/banana.

5:00 — Evening segment. Sit in traffic.

5:30–8:00 — Attend class.

8:15–8:30 — Drive home.

8:30–9:00 — Prepare dinner and eat.

9:00–10:30 — Watch TV.

10:30 — Return to bed.

I can see how the ordered calm of my life could look like heaven to people who live in constant turbulence, but what I felt when I was living it was hell. I'd returned from that rafting trip infected with what I now call "My Joy." It's a disease that destroyed one life but gave birth to another. But back then I didn't know what to call it; I was just confused. I walked around in my gray, slope-shouldered, baggy life depressed and frustrated. I raged at my husband and I wept to my friends. I cried heaving sobs at what I saw as the waste of my life. I had just seen myself in full exuberance, in free-falling happiness: I had really taken advantage of my good health, my family, of this glorious planet with its wandering streams, brilliant blue skies and thunderous clouds. But back in the office, I simply saw myself inhabiting routines, blah-blah-blahing in endless meetings, going to birthday parties, giving housewarming gifts, buying groceries, lamenting traffic, paying bills, feeding myself, my husband and the three cats.

All I could think about was getting out. That's when I started a new folder on my computer called "Escape." I started amassing endless, ranting journal entries, I wrote and mailed letters to outdoor companies applying for jobs, any job, from cashier to stable hand, if it was associated with an outdoor industry. Friends, co-workers and family tried to counsel me. My husband despaired at my restlessness. In cheerful tones people told me, "Well, yes, it's hard to come back from a good vacation and get back into the grind, but what else can you do?"

To me, they sounded like people who had given up. I'd answer fever-ishly, "But wait, is this any way to live, from vacation to vacation? Is that really what we're doing here on this planet? Is that it?"

I guess I was having an existential crisis. I'd seen people in college con-front these issues, usually with a bong close at hand, surrounded by a bunch of other similarly confused, contemplative pals. I was too obsessed at that time with getting into a good sorority or having this-or-that boy think I was cute to think about anything as heavy as the mean-ing of life. This now was my awakening.

I decided to fight. I made the decision not to get back into the grind like everyone said I should. I examined every aspect of my life and thought about whether it was something that made me happy or not.

> "In the white heat of panic about the direction of my life, I didn't care about anything else except saving myself."

Then I started running like a mad-woman toward the things I came to know could make me happy.

My husband, frustrated with my brash decisions and rude behavior, said angrily one day on his way out of town for a weekend, "You do realize, don't you, what effect all this is going to have on our marriage?" In a way, I did realize. I admit now that I was very selfish. But at the same time, none of these repercus-sions seemed to matter to me. I was focused on keeping "My Joy" alive. I began to see everyone in Washington, D.C., including my husband, as a lost drone, while every-one in the Grand Canyon looked enlightened and open to life. In the white heat of panic about the direction of my life, I didn't care about anything else except saving myself.

Eventually one of the letters in my "Escape" folder got a response. I had found a river company owner in Idaho who said he'd host me for a few weeks of river experiences in exchange for some general business advice. As it turned out, even though I had been a corporate business consultant for seven years, I had never done any consulting with a small business before. I had become such a cog in my consulting career that everything had been oriented around the process, not the results. In my meetings with the river company owner, I would listen intently, trying to understand his problems and attempting to translate my well honed career experiences into something useful for his business challenges. In the final analysis, I learned more from him and his wife than they learned from me.

I decided after that wonderful summer to start my own company. I would offer consulting services to businesses in the adventure travel industry. I named my company Xola, which means "stay in peace" in Xhosa, Nelson Mandela's language. I was thinking of my own peace when I came up with that name, but I now see peace in a much broader context of the sense of peace and awareness that the outdoors can bring. Xola now has a network of consultants, and we work in countries around the world, supporting governments that want to develop adventure tourism markets. Our work with small businesses helps strengthen rural economies and encourages environmental conservation. It's a new kind of peace we have been inventing, and every day I wake up happy and excited about what "My Joy" can do in the world at large.

And when I get scared, as I often do, I think back to that river trip that started me on the path to my joy. I dredge up the guide's voice and the way he had of talking through those long and thrilling but frightening rapids. I know I'm giving my best effort to make a meaningful contribution, and I'm building a company that provides a platform for others to do the same.

Christina Heyniger is the president of Xola Consulting, Inc., and an associate with the Adventure Travel Trade Association. Her travel writing can be found online and in *Riding the Hulahula to the Arctic Ocean: A Guide to Fifty Extraordinary Adventures for the Seasoned Traveler*. Originally from Anchorage, Alaska, Christina now lives in Santa Fe, New Mexico.

True Nature

Barbara Blossom Ashmun

A Bronx apartment was no place for a gardener to bloom. Like a seed dropped into a dark, dry place, my true nature lay dormant. Closed up tight as a bud in winter, I protected myself from my family's strict rules: my first-generation Orthodox Jewish parents expected me to marry a nice Jewish boy and raise children. Yet early signs of my gardening future cropped up all along the way. When I was 19, I spent a year in Israel, and while there I kept a journal for the first time. "Sitting on our table is a vase full of poppies," I wrote, "each one wide open, red velvety petals fuzzily downed on the outside, deep blue centers well exposed. Beside them a jar full of cyclamen, shooting up with tips pinked. My heart brims."

In my first Manhattan apartment, when my boyfriend brought me a trailing pothos plant with marbled leaves as a housewarming present, I felt my little place become a home. Years later, when I moved in with my husband Ray, I asked him to build shelves inside the frames of our tall French windows. I grew African violets and Swedish ivy in the milky light of Manhattan's Upper West Side. But at this time drug-related violence was rampant in New York City. One tragic night Ray's cousin was shot dead. Shocked, we sprang into action and made plans to leave the city.

I applied to Portland State University for a master's program in social work and was accepted. By then I was thirty. Ray and I lived in an apartment with a little terrace, where I grew my first red geraniums in paper pulp pots. Ray found a market research job, I went to classes and made new friends. Life seemed to be flowing along smoothly, when an unexpected jolt shook us. My favorite aunt died of a heart attack. During her lifetime, Libby gave me many gifts — my first visit to the theater, my first ice cream sundae, my first real leather purse. And when she died, she left me a gift that changed my life forever: enough money for a down payment on a house with a garden.

Somehow, without any experience, I took to that place as if I were born to garden. Playing in the soil was as addictive as chocolate. I took ownership by clearing the site. I yanked out gloomy old cedars and peeled away sod to make room for flower beds. Planting peonies and daylilies, I put down my own new roots in that garden.

When I graduated, we celebrated with a visit to Butchart Gardens in Victoria, British Columbia. I brought back seed packets — larkspur and clarkia, godetia and marigolds. With the help of a neighbor, I began my education as a gardener, learning everything I could. How to start seeds in damp sphagnum moss. How to make a compost pile. How to plant tomatoes deep, and pinch out the suckers. How to tie them to stakes with remnants of his wife's old stockings. How to water, weed and prune. I grew into a gardener.

But professional life called. With my new social work degree, I got a job at Emanuel Hospital, helping patients and families start over after strokes, head injuries and burns. At first I loved the challenge, but within a year I dreaded going to work. My mornings in the rehabilitation center felt like bad dreams. When I opened the door to the place, the smell of sickness hit me. Old people confined to wheelchairs moaned, "Let me out of here," over and over. Stroke patients learning to walk again navigated the halls with physical therapists trailing behind, holding onto their belts to stabilize them. The Burn Unit where I spent afternoons was even worse. Patients here had serious burns from house fires, electrical accidents, and car crashes. My heart went out to them. The bandage-wrapped mummies, the faces without noses, and the amputated limbs were horrifying. Smells of decaying skin, of stinging betadine, of my own sweat as I roasted in my gown and mask, filled my nose. Inside my mind, *I* was the one screaming *Get me out of here!*

If work was a nightmare, my personal life was a horror movie. Out of the blue, Ray decided to leave. "I don't want to be married anymore," he announced one Saturday morning. Stunned, I could hardly speak. All my questions—why now, what happened, can't we talk this over— were met with silence. He moved out.

My only refuge was the garden. Each day after work I drove home and threw off clothes reeking of the hospital. I pulled on jeans and a T-shirt and headed outside. Kneeling on the soft lawn, I inhaled the smells of damp soil and green grass, the delicious aroma of lily-of-the-valley, and the minty scent of rosemary. Like a transfusion, the freshness of plants restored me to life.

I agonized about quitting my job, hesitant to give up a career with a decent salary and good benefits. When I talked to my mother, she pressed me to stay. "How can you think of giving it up and throwing away your Master's degree," she said, "especially now that you're divorced!"

The picture of me heaving that framed degree out the window both excited and terrified me. At work I watched the land- scape gardeners through the window. I longed to be in their yellow slickers and tall green boots, join them raking leaves into big piles. One morning, while inter- viewing a patient, I imagined crawling into the bed, then throwing her out on the floor. Shocked by my fantasy, I faced the facts. It was time to quit. That night I wrote down all my expenses and figured out how much money it would take to buy myself one year of freedom. I resolved to

> "Somehow, without any experience, I took to that place as if I were born to garden. Playing in the soil was as addictive as chocolate."

save, then resign. That meant no more new clothing, movies or dinners out. Making a plan lifted a huge weight off my shoulders. But it took two years to save enough. Meanwhile, I worried. Was I making a big mistake by giving up a secure job? Could I pay the mortgage and put food on the table?

Then a friend said the magic words that set me straight:

"How much is your peace of mind worth?"

With Ray gone, I had no one to consider but myself. If I risked a new start and failed, so be it. As Janis Joplin sang, "Freedom's just another word for nothing left to lose." My marriage was over, my social work career was killing me. It was time to break free.

Finally, I quit my job and jumped into my new life with boundless enthusiasm. I enrolled in landscape design classes at Rock Creek Community College, in horticulture classes at Clark College, and signed up for Master Gardener classes. I joined the Rose Society, the Iris Society, the Lily Society, the Rock Garden Society, the Hardy Plant Society. My horticulture teacher allowed me to design and plant a perennial border for the campus. Anyone with eyes could see that I had found my true path, but I couldn't yet see it. To me, gardening was still just a passionate hobby. I didn't understand it was my life until I took a class called Life Work Planning at Marylhurst University. When we were asked to describe a perfect day, I wrote about the day I designed that border at Clark College.

At our last class, one of the students asked me to design her front yard for $100. My mouth fell open, and I said "Yes!" Without any fanfare, she had catapulted me into my new career. With my teacher's encouragement and a graphic designer's help, I printed up business cards and launched my new business, Creative Garden Design.

Every artist needs a bread and butter job, and luckily a new friend in my landscape design class told me Portland General Electric needed someone to maintain their indoor plants after business hours. Perfect!

That job left me free to design gardens during the day. Everywhere I went, helping hands reached out, and I grabbed them. A former social work colleague encouraged me to teach gardening classes. First I taught a two-week class on bulbs, then a four-week class on perennials. Eventually I taught six- and eight-week classes, on garden design, roses, trees. Small steps led to more branches on my path. I photographed many gardens and created slide shows for classes, garden shows and garden clubs. I planted and groomed hundreds of red geraniums and purple heliotropes in beds glowing with color. I ransacked greenhouses in three counties to find the most colorful flowers for a show garden, where many corporate parties were held.

Marsha Sinetar's *Do What You Love and the Money Will Follow* hadn't been published yet, but I could have been her poster girl. I began to trust the process: work hard at what I love, connect with like-minded people, and I would always have enough. I gardened for two more estate gardens, and kept teaching and designing. I wrote a gardening column for *The Woman's Journal*, a local paper. That led to more and more writing about gardening, and I marked my fiftieth year by being published in *Fine Gardening*.

I can now declare myself a professional gardening writer. But I'm still a gardener! Each morning I write, glancing occasionally out the picture window which frames the garden. Each afternoon I garden, tending the plants that inspire me. Nearly thirty years since I jumped into the unknown, I treasure my fully reinvented life.

Barbara Blossom Ashmun is the author of six books, including *Married to My Garden* and *Garden Retreats: Creating an Outdoor Sanctuary*. Her garden column appears weekly in the *Portland Tribune*, and thousands of visitors have enjoyed her own garden since 1986.

Vision Takes Flight

Sybil Erden

I always told people that I had an invisible sign over my home, a sign that could only be seen by animals:

"Sucker Lives Here. Look Pathetic for Food."

Since leaving my parents' home in my young adulthood, lost and stray cats and dogs would find their way to my house, and I would either find their owner, find them a new home or keep them. I always knew that animals would be in my life. But I never would have imagined that someday they would *be* my life.

I've always considered myself to be a very motivated, disciplined and creative person, someone who views creativity as the expression of my spirituality. For almost 25 years I worked as an artist, painting, creating photographs, drawings and montages and showing my work extensively. I was quite successful, and by my mid-thirties no longer had to work outside jobs to support myself. To my friends, and perhaps even to myself, it seemed like a life no one would want to change.

Then, when I was in my early forties, I began volunteering my artistic skills to benefit St. Mary's Food Bank in Phoenix, Arizona. From there I went around the country and ultimately to the former Soviet Union documenting hunger-related issues. While in Russia and the Ukraine, I couldn't help but notice the plight of the many animals that were being tossed into the streets. It tore at my heart. I returned home at the

Sybil Erden

end of summer with pockets grease-stained from carrying scraps of food for these helpless creatures.

Upon returning to the U.S., I educated myself about the harsh realities faced by companion animals, and was horrified to discover how that approximately 7.5 million animals were lost to neglect each year. By now I was living on an acre of property in central Phoenix and my menagerie included cats, dogs, sheep, a donkey, llamas, chickens, guinea fowl, and a growing number of companion birds. I went online and began to see that there was an unrecognized overpopulation problem with caged birds, much the same as with cats and dogs. I love birds. I love their songs, their color, their intelligence and spirit. I found myself taking in more and more unwanted parrots. By 1995, two years after that trip abroad, I had over 60 birds in residence.

Having worked with various non-profits since the late 1970's, and with (at that time) a sustainable income from my artwork and investments, I became resolved to found a sanctuary for captive birds, primarily parrots. In 1997, The Oasis Sanctuary was born in my backyard. The Oasis was the first life-care facility primarily for parrots to be approved as a tax exempt organization by the IRS. At the end of 1997 there were 100 birds in residence.

With our resident population growing, we needed more space. At the end of 2000, with 250 birds in tow, we moved to our current location on 72 acres in Cascabel, Arizona, outside the small town of Benson in the southeastern corner of the state. Today we have 700 birds in residence. We have grown from a budget of $20,000 in 1998 to over $600,000 for 2009. We currently have 10 full-time paid staff members. In 1999 The Oasis was accredited by the American Sanctuary Association, and we are also accredited by the Global Federation of Sanctuaries.

> "I see all of my life's works to be part of a spiritual journey— leaving the place just a wee bit better than I found it, even though I am aware that my human footprint will slowly be washed away by time."

In spite of my passion for these birds, this growth hasn't always been easy for me. The greatest change and challenge has been working with other people. It's one thing to work alone in the studio, and another to work with staff, the board, volunteers and donors. It has also been a financial burden. I've put literally everything I have into this project, and am left without any savings to support my old age. While that is somewhat frightening, I am content with the knowledge that through my efforts and those of others who have helped, a safe haven for animals has been created. Yes, it has cost me in terms of time, toil and finances. But this experience has both enriched my spirit and humbled me. I wouldn't trade it for anything.

Since I undertook this journey, I am 15 years older, calmer, and certainly more tired. It's very different working for one's self as an artist than for a "greater good" as founder of a non-profit. Although I view The Oasis Sanctuary as still in its infancy, the work we do has helped change the face of "aviculture," and we are helping to make the world a more humane place for birds. That sense of tangible accomplishment is worth so very much.

I see all of my life's works to be part of a spiritual journey—leaving the place just a wee bit better than I found it, even though I am fully aware that my human footprint will slowly be washed away by time. As for my creative side, I spend a lot of time writing: replying to e-mail from around the country and the world as well as writing about the issues surrounding captive birds in our country. I have done very few paintings in the years since I undertook this mission, although I do look forward to getting back to some work in the studio as time permits. Perhaps The Oasis Sanctuary is actually the largest piece of artwork, if you will, that I have endeavored to create. When I hear the calls of its many avian inhabitants, I am embraced by the beauty of The Oasis, and I am so glad I took this new direction in my life.

Sybil Erden was born in New York City to parents who immigrated to the United States after World War II. Since 1998 she has traveled the country speaking about the plight of captive parrots. She lives in the wilds of southern Arizona with her partner Jeff and their menagerie.

Of Science and Self

Hayley Boesky

All my life I thought *the* question, *the* quest was: what is it we're all doing here? What is this planet, what is this point in time and how did it all come to be? My curiosity for a satisfactory explanation of our being was the most compelling force in my life, and it launched me down a long, circuitous road.

My quest began at the University of Pennsylvania, where I majored in mathematics, the tool for decoding the mysteries of the universe. The Chairman of the Astrophysics Department discouraged me from pursuing a second major in astrophysics since, according to him, it was not a field for women. But I would not be discouraged. Fortunately, he went on sabbatical during my senior year and the standing chair approved my second major in astrophysics.

Penn also had a social science requirement. First I tried communications, and I hated it. Then, I tried linguistics, and I hated it. To me, these were not science by any stretch of the imagination. My mind works in black and white, and I grew frustrated by the subjectivity, the grey shades, of these fields.

Then, I discovered economics. Like communications and linguistics, it was considered a social science. But to me, economics was an application of the quantitative skills that I was learning on the math side of my major. I found it to be fun and gratifying to apply these skills to tangible, everyday problems. My math skills now became a vehicle for me

Hayley Boesky

to learn about other disciplines, helping to open the world of economics, which I found fascinating. Soon I found myself auditing courses in finance. Through the economics and finance courses I was taking, the calculus class I was teaching to Wharton students, and the vast social network at Penn, I made lots of connections with students who went on to pursue careers in finance.

I graduated from college in 1988— the spring after Black Tuesday and a tough year for business students to get jobs on Wall Street. However, I was fortunate to have several options. For a year, I worked as a pension consultant at a large firm. While at this firm, my bosses told me that if I passed certain actuarial exams—which, with my math background looked pretty easy—I'd earn bonuses—money to go back to school to study anything I wanted. So I started taking actuarial exams and graduate classes in math at New York University.

Soon I was offered a fellowship in astrophysics at Columbia University, and the prospect of getting paid to pursue my dream of studying the mysteries of the universe was too exciting to turn down. Unfortunately, much of my work was done in an attic at Columbia University on 120th Street, or in the Andes in northern Chile at 14,000 feet, and after four or five years, I came to feel isolated and lonely. It didn't suit my personality. I needed to be more collaborative, more interactive.

In my fifth year of graduate school, I was invited to an astrophysics conference in Israel with others in the field: something like 21 people showed up. Nonetheless, it was exciting to interact and share ideas with others. But when I came home, I felt a tremendous sense of letdown.

That, I think was my moment of revelation. I realized then, that I would be working virtually alone again for another six years, until the next conference—that even when I coauthored papers, my colleagues and I would collaborate via email and I'd never actually meet them. I had to admit that, as much as I l liked the study of astrophysics, the field didn't like me. It simply didn't suit my personality. It was time for a change.

When I realized I wanted to leave astrophysics, I started auditing courses at the business school and investigating careers in the financial sector. I was afraid to admit to anybody in the astrophysics department at Columbia that I was thinking about doing something different. I was worried about how my professors would react if they knew that I didn't want to stay the course, since professors invest a lot in their students (at least mine did). Ultimately, though, I think they were relieved. My advisor wanted me to be happy and saw that the lifestyle didn't suit me well. During my final years in graduate school, I think he was as worried about me as I was. This decision to make the leap from astrophysics to finance was not about the money; I didn't mind living paycheck to paycheck as an academic, knowing I'd only have only a few dollars left in my account at the end of every month. Changing fields was a matter of finding a place that suited my personality, the skills I had to offer, who I was, and a constantly challenging environment with colleagues who would help me continue to learn.

> "When I took the job, I had no idea that the entire global financial system was going to reach the brink of disaster."

I started calling my contacts, my friends, people I knew who were working on Wall Street. I asked them if I could sit with them in their workplace to observe. I wanted to understand better the distinction between bankers, traders and analysts and see how they spent their time on a day-to-day basis. But when it came time to get a job, I didn't go back to my contacts; I wanted to feel like all of the hard work that I put into earning my degrees was worth something. Looking back, I see how naïve I was—I simply sent my resume to various HR people. Fortunately, though, my CV was unique enough to capture attention and a job, and I went from the isolation of the lab right to the training floor of Goldman Sachs. Culture shock. But I loved the energy and pace of it.

At Goldman, I was fortunate enough to find a terrific mentor and a culture that suited me well, and I worked there for nine years. After Goldman, I went to work at a hedge fund, but didn't find it to be rewarding in a meaningful way. I had better work/life balance and was paid well, but it just wasn't very gratifying to me. I yearned to make a difference in a meaningful way. A former (and now current) Treasury official suggested that I meet a guy named Tim Geithner at the New York Fed. I hadn't heard of Tim and I didn't consider the New York Fed to be the center of policy making (In fact I'd always thought of it as a rather sleepy place), but based on the tremendous respect I had for this individual, and the logistical convenience of the Federal Reserve Bank of New York, I decided to take his advice.

Within minutes of meeting Tim, I was blown away. I was immediately impressed by his intensity, his ability to process information and to quickly grasp the heart of issues which were novel to him. I knew he would be an incredible person to work for. One thing that I have learned from both my academic and professional experiences, is that who you work for is as critical as what you do. Clearly Tim would be a fantastic role model and an inspiring leader. So I went to work for the New York Fed as Vice President of Capital Markets, Analysis and Trading.

When I took the job, I obviously had no idea that the entire global financial system was going to reach the brink of disaster. Throughout the crisis, the hours of work that were put in by me and my colleagues at Fed were astounding. For a long period, it was not a rare event for us to work straight through the night and the following days.

I remember the infamous Lehman/AIG weekend. I was at work Thursday night until five in the morning; I went home to shower, dress and return to the Bank. Expecting to get home early that day, I figured I'd wear a new pair of 4-inch high heels I had purchased as a sympathy gift for myself. I went back to work by 7 A.M., and didn't come home until Sunday night. I had those brand new 4-inch heels on for over 60 hours. It was an incredible stretch, and the weekend was so intense I never once realized how much pain my feet were in.

Markets have calmed since then, but for us it's still incredibly busy; we still have a lot of work ahead of us, and the hours are still long. It's been tough at home, with the amount of time and energy my work requires of me. Tough for the kids, for my husband, and for me. So far, it hasn't gotten any easier.

It's interesting; as we dive into the unemployment numbers we are dealing with today, we hear a lot of men just saying, "I can't find a job that's going to pay me in a way I can support my family," and leaving it at that. On the other hand, we might also be seeing a lot of women stepping up and saying, "I'm going to reinvent myself" and retraining for new jobs. The numbers are noticeable: men are exiting the work force at a significantly faster pace than women.

As far as my next career move goes, I don't know exactly what I'm going to do. I am open minded. It will be difficult to match the excitement and intensity and import of the past few years. But maybe that's a good thing. One thing I guarantee: I will end up someplace where I'll be able to come home for dinner at least once a week.

As I look back on the quest I began so long ago, I marvel at the twisting route it has taken. I look at the road that lies ahead, and I know one thing: there are no easy answers. But I've also learned that the satisfaction, the joy, the excitement, the challenge—they are all in the quest.

Hayley Boesky joined the Federal Reserve Bank of New York in 2007 as a Vice President and Director of Market Analysis after working at Moore Capital Management and Goldman Sachs investment bank. She holds a doctorate in astrophysics from Columbia University. She also earned Masters degrees in science and philosophy from Columbia University, where she served on the Board of the Graduate School of Arts and Science from 2000 to 2003.

The View from Here

Bari Nan Cohen

I may be genetically predisposed for lifestyle and life-altering change. I was raised in a small mountain town in Vermont by parents who had moved there from Washington, DC. The opportunities for wholesome, outdoor activity were not lost on them, and they made sure we took advantage of everything life in Vermont had to offer—alpine and cross-country skiing and ice skating in winter, horseback riding and tennis lessons in summer. Plus, we traveled to big cities to expose my sister and me to theater, music and dance. These trips only whetted my appetite to move to New York City when I grew up. I devoured trashy novels that featured career-driven single women in the city.

In high school, I started dating a guy I met on a summer bus tour of the country who happened to live in New York. Our "dates" were weekends spent at each other's family's houses. On his trips to see me, we skied. On my trips to see him, we hopped the Long Island Rail Road into the city and went exploring—walking the city end to end, standing in line for "twofers" at Duffy Square, wandering through FAO Schwarz and Tower Records. I was hooked, not only on the city I'd always fantasized about, but on this guy who had as much energy for exploring as I did.

We carried on this long-distance courtship across several state lines, and, at one point, the Atlantic Ocean and a couple of continents. And yet we remained each other's constant, confidant, anchor. Our rela-

Bari Nan Cohen

tionship allowed each of us the freedom to explore what we needed in college, to make friends without the minute-to-minute intensity of an on-campus relationship, and share those friends with each other when we visited on weekends.

We were—and still are—crazy about each other. We embraced each other's ambitions and had a great time encouraging each other and talking about it all on the phone. We found ways to be together without smothering each other—weekends at each other's colleges—mine outside Boston, his in Rochester, New York. We eagerly anticipated my graduation from college, so that I could join him in New York and we could embark on our next set of adventures, this time side-by-side.

Everything went according to plan. I hit the ground running in New York. The first year was a blur as I got my start working in magazines, and Jeff began working in his family's business. We rented an apartment in Queens and a year into our lease started looking for a place to buy. We moved into Manhattan and climbed the next rungs of our career ladders. We spent every weekend at open houses in Brooklyn and Manhattan trying to figure out where we'd move when we needed something bigger. On a lark, we moved back to Queens a couple of years later, to a townhouse with a little green space. We got a puppy. We spent an inordinate amount of time leaving New York for weekend escapes to Vermont; vacations with friends on cruises; even an impulsive weekend trip to Rome.

On many of these trips, we'd wonder what it would be like to live in these places. It sounded like so much harmless fantasizing, but there was an underlying urgency to the conversations that neither of us was willing to acknowledge. The seams were coming apart at Jeff's job. My job satisfaction was generally good, but the higher I climbed on the masthead, the more meetings I needed to attend, and the less time I had for the work I actually enjoyed. I wasn't complaining, the work was fun, the colleagues were great, but I found myself, midwinter, ruining my shoes on slushy sidewalks and missing the more bucolic settings I'd lived in before.

Still, we put down roots. We renovated. We talked about which room would be the nursery, because we'd finally built up the courage to decide to try. Just one more vacation with cocktails and dreams and we'd go for it. It was Jeff's 30th birthday.

It was all precipices that week. Of course it was: it was a ski trip. I'd never been so high. Up. I'd never skied anywhere but Vermont. And here I was, in the mountains of Utah, skiing intermediate terrain at an altitude I'd never experienced, and finding myself on the edges of drops they would have called "expert" back home. But if I felt intimidated by the terrain, I took it as a sign that it was time to conquer. That week, I found new ski legs. New confidence. And a new home. I sat on a chairlift next to my husband—and made a declaration:

"I don't want to ski five days a year. I want to ski five days a week. Fix it."

"Okay, let's move here."

"Okay. Let's."

"I mean it."

"Me too."

"Really."

It was done. We jumped off the precipice. We moved within months. We handled the shock-and-awe syndrome with our families. We endured all the "Are you crazy" intervention talks from colleagues and friends. We held hands and hoped we were making the right decision. Yes, there was a lot of talk of pushing limits, exiting the comfort zone and trying new things. In many ways, the security of having a partner with whom to do this gave me a wide enough comfort zone to push the limits.

But at the same time, we realized our marriage itself was at a crossroads. Jeff was unhappy enough in his work situation, which was tied into his family relationships, that the sadness and difficulty had encroached on our relationship. We both knew it. He asked me to give him some courage before he broke the news of our move to his family. I looked him directly in the eye and said, "I'm going to Park City. Are you coming?" It was all he needed to hear. "Yup. Okay, I'm good. I'm with you."

I was, at 28, a senior editor at a well-respected national magazine. No one expected me to hop off the fast track—least of all, me. But I could not resist the lure of the mountains, the promise of a lifestyle a bit closer to the way I was raised, blended with the more cosmopolitan one I'd chosen almost simultaneously with choosing my husband. Park City had the small-town feel, plus, there was a real city with cultural opportunities and an international airport just 30 minutes to the west. And skiing. So much good skiing. I wanted to claim this. I uttered the phrase "lifestyle change," with annoying frequency. But I meant it. I felt emboldened. Like this could be the first of many changes. I could become a yoga instructor. We could move to Seattle. Or Singapore. Well, maybe not Singapore, but the very idea that change could beget change was an endorphin rush all its own.

In the mountains, I got a charge out of pushing myself. How many sports could I fit into a day? Hiking in the morning, biking in the afternoon, nine holes of golf at dusk? Why not? When I flew back to New York for some meetings in my new capacity as Editor-at-Large at the magazine that had employed me prior to the move, I made the conscious decision to wear a skirt that would show off the bruises I'd earned on a mountain biking trail. Badges of honor. Outward examples of the inward change.

Yet, that inward change was hard to chart. When you're used to following a path because others expect you to, and because you expect it of yourself, and you're not quite sure how much those depend upon each other, it's easy to lose your footing. It took me a while to cut ties with New York. Part of me wanted to believe we could live in both places at once. We didn't have a local hair stylist or dentist for the first two years. We were flying back frequently enough that we kept those appointments on their usual schedules. We bumped up against political differences, and even cultural missteps when we stepped outside the circle of "expat New Yorkers" we'd found here. Yet it was all the more fun to navigate because we were doing it together. Plus, I didn't, for a second, have to give up my girlhood career dreams. That part only got better.

> "We held hands and hoped we were making the right decision. But at the same time, we realized our marriage itself was at a crossroads..."

I was sought out by former colleagues who valued the creative space I occupied, literally and figuratively. They understood that my flexibility meant I could work more productively. If I felt blocked on a writing assignment, or had done all I could do to set up a celebrity interview and was still stalled, I took myself out for a snowshoe hike, cleared my head and returned to the work refreshed and, perhaps, possessed of an a-ha moment to approach the stall in a different way.

Today, I feel like I have claimed the life I didn't even know to dream of: growing up, I thought I had to choose between idyllic surroundings and a big-time career. I'm an editor at a national magazine (in part because I had the experience and the guts to suggest to the editors there that I could do a staff job at a New York-based company from my perch in the mountains), who hikes or skis on her lunch break, and takes full advantage of the wi-fi in the RV campgrounds we frequent on the weekends. There's something very centering about fulfilling my wanderlust by exploring the West with my husband and our two kids and our two dogs in a motor home. We often say there's a certain comfort to be had in knowing we're all together in whatever the day's adventure brings—it's the same rush I used to get hopping between stores and museums in New York City, but it's only been enriched by the experience of seeing what our kids discover on these trips.

In a way, the success of this life is in the fact that I'm secure in the knowledge that having a partner who shares my vision for a big life, who knows we're partners in this big life, makes it possible to both plan and not to plan. There is security in that. But I'm also secure in the knowledge that should that plan change, and we find ourselves at another crossroads, we know the solid ground isn't specific to this location—it's wherever we stand together.

Bari Nan Cohen is the proud mother of two boys, the spoiled wife of a great cook, and an avid skier, hiker and RV traveler. She spends her weekends playing out her fantasy of being "Julie McCoy, Your Cruise Director," and her weekdays interviewing celebrities in her role as Entertainment Editor at *Good Housekeeping Magazine*. She lives with her family and their two dogs in Park City, Utah.

Becoming Me

Melissa A. Slaybaugh

Everyone tells me I am constantly reinventing myself, but I never really think of it that way. I think reinvention is an outside perspective–the way others see me, not as I see myself. To me, my life is an ever-growing, ever-changing journey. Sometimes it's meant changing careers; sometimes it's meant changing what's inside me; and sometimes it's just meant changing my perspective. No, I have never looked at my life as reinventing myself. It is all just a continuation of me.

I've always been good with numbers, and I started working in banking just out of high school. It was a necessity and part of my initial game plan, my only game plan. I had no money for college, a family I was eager to leave and from whom I received no useful support, and a long life ahead of me. The bank I chose was willing to pay my tuition, so I went to work there as a teller.

I finished college and quickly moved up the ladder in banking, constantly asking for greater challenges and being rewarded in kind. As soon as I got as far as I could in one bank, I moved to the next, eventually working my way up to Vice President in charge of major operations in a large commercial bank. I had no particular career plan, just the innate sense that I needed to be challenged and could always do more. I was well respected and known as the go-to person to handle tough situations. People viewed me as smart, successful, ambitious, and motivated. But it was so much simpler than that: in truth, I was bored easily and needed continual challenge in my work life to keep me moving forward.

After working my way up the corporate ladder in banking, I found myself closing in on my thirtieth birthday. As that landmark approached, I started feeling that much was missing from my life, that I could do more, be a better person and, mostly, know myself more fully. One thing I did know: I no longer wanted to be a banker. It had served its purpose, which had been to give me something stable and secure. Now, I was ready to move on to a new challenge. So, after ten years and quite a bit of outward success, I quit.

People thought I was crazy to walk away from the success I had achieved at a young age in such a solid industry, but I knew I was moving into the next phase of my life. I was not reinventing myself, but continuing my journey. For the next couple of years, I did short-term consulting projects–six months here, three months there. I worked on everything from accounting to computer programming to project management. I didn't want to be locked into anything too permanent or distracting. I focused on myself, on understanding what motivated me and made me tick.

> "Many things I was searching for on my journey have been intangible things that were within me from the beginning—I just needed to find them."

This period was fraught with difficult emotional realizations that challenged me to change and become a better and more whole person. In fact, it turned out to be a period of tremendous growth. Having come from a severely challenged childhood, I'd never had the luxury of focusing on myself. I'd never had the chance to take the time to think deeply and to feel deeply. During this time, my friends saw me as changing significantly, but I was actually becoming more of myself, understanding myself better and living a deeper, more emotional life.

Importantly, during this time I reconnected with my love of cooking and entertaining. To me, this was a natural step in my journey to get more in touch with myself and what brings me joy, because cooking is such an emotional thing to me. I began to become interested in new, creative ways of preparing food and putting menus together. It became my art, my creative outlet. I started experimenting with different kinds of regional cooking and expanded my knowledge of the alchemic possibilities that could be achieved with herbs and spices. I learned everything I could about creative food preparation.

In the meantime, I tired of continually looking for new consulting work and was looking for a more secure job back in banking. Then a serendipitous opportunity fell into my lap: the chance to work for an international financial services consulting firm. I could travel the world, utilize my banking expertise, and be continually challenged by new clients and a variety of projects, and actually make a difference by implementing meaningful enhancements to banking organizations. At the same time, I would have the opportunity to learn about different cultures, local culinary flavors, specialties and preparations. When I went food shopping or browsed gourmet shops in other countries where I didn't know the native language, I frequently had to use creatively descriptive hand gestures, but I managed to leave with the foods I wanted. Clearly, this career shift allowed me to have some fun and adventure as well as continue my private, more personal journey.

Nevertheless, no matter how well I planned this phase, life intervened to change those plans. Shortly after I began working at the consulting firm, I met the woman who would become my life partner. The idea of spending my life with someone was a new concept to me that I had never before really considered, but one that I recognized the moment I laid eyes on her. My heart was finally open and she crept right in. A new, unexpected journey or "reinvention" began—one that would change my life in profound ways.

I had already learned how to open my heart, but the next leg of my journey was learning how to be truly intimate and to let someone into my life. I went into this phase with wild abandon. It was confusing, exciting and difficult. My partner and I eventually left the consulting firm to begin our own consulting practice. We started it from nothing and built it into a successful business. Although working together day in, day out created its own challenges, it forced us to work through our intimacy issues. You can be sure this was not easy. It took quite a bit of time, angst and fortitude, but we were determined to move forward together, so we boosted each other along.

My "reinvention" had taken on yet a whole new meaning that I never before could have anticipated. Being in an intimate relationship that merged both our work and home lives was new emotional territory and I was determined to get through it with a greater sense of wholeness. Not only did we have to confront work-related issues such as clients, sales and finances together, but we also piled on a dog, moving to a different state and buying a home. Together we experienced deaths, births, marriages, redefining family, etc. I spent time cooking as one of my forms of relaxation, and we entertained quite a bit. Although cooking always came to me naturally, I attended boot camp at the Culinary Institute to further hone my cooking skills.

After over thirteen years of consulting and a continually solid relationship, I started feeling the same restlessness I felt when I left banking. I knew there was still more ahead. I had continued on my path of self-examination, reflection and personal growth, so by the time I reached 50, I had a pretty good idea of who I was as a person, what I was good at and what I enjoyed doing. The next leg of my journey would have to involve every facet of my life up to that point.

Now, at 52 and with a strong relationship to support me, I have given up my consulting business and am propelling myself in a new direction. I've put my passion for cooking and entertaining together with my other skills and am creating a cooking-related web business. Once again, I am building something from the ground up. The business will incorporate my strong cooking skills, my management and business skills and my financial aptitude. It will let me manage my own time and do something new each and every day, to engage with people at my own pace, and to enjoy the luxury of sharing my cooking expertise with a wider audience. It will also give me a daily creative outlet that I have never enjoyed in any of my business endeavors before. It will bring together my emotional life, my creative life and my business life, all in one place. The website will showcase both unique recipes and simple foods and link them together for dinner parties and consecutive meals in such an organized manner that cooking and entertaining become accessible to everyone, free of anxiety and mayhem. I have become "The Accessible Chef." The idea that I can combine the passion I once thought was just a hobby with my business skills and experience, and make a career out of it all, is the most exciting, fulfilling thing I can imagine. My professional life is now not only my vocation but my avocation as well.

As I move toward my sixth decade, I realize that many things I was searching for on my journey have been intangible things that were within me from the beginning—I just needed to find them. The people around me scratch their heads and wonder why I have given up two successful careers. But I know I am not reinventing myself or going on an unrelated trajectory. Rather, I am pushing myself further forward and becoming more of who I really am and always have been.

Melissa A. Slaybaugh lives in Connecticut with her partner and their yellow Labrador retriever. She is the founder of The Accessible Chef, www.TheAccessibleChef.com.

Celebrant

Celia Milton

During every wedding ceremony I perform, I say that life often hands us gifts when we least expect them, and very often when we're most desperate for them. All we need are open hands, an open heart and an open mind to see the possibilities that the universe offers us. Then *our* work begins!

My life, love and work have always been inseparably and happily entwined. Together with my husband, (who became my ex-husband but still business partner), I owned a catering and event planning company for almost 20 years. It was the backdrop for many of my significant relationships.

Our catering company orchestrated celebrations that marked the spiritual and emotional rituals illuminating our clients' lives, from humble church hall christenings to grandiose backyard weddings. I had a fascinating and frenetic career happily entangled in these ceremonies, and I learned from every one. I can make Passover charoset; I can lead the Chicken Dance. I traveled with birthday candles, wedding cake servers, yarmulkes and at least 200 feet of extension cord. I was never bored; I was often inspired.

Even though it was hard to be enthusiastic about unloading catering vans at 3 A.M. and scraping guacamole out of the musical equipment, I never seriously contemplated a change. Then our catering company

Celia Milton

won a contract to cater a party at the church I'd gone to almost every Sunday until I left home for college. Trying to put a staff together, I called every waiter I knew, with no success. I finally realized I'd have to cater it myself.

In spite of the hard work, I thoroughly enjoyed the event. I had the opportunity to hear the sermon, and the minister was brilliant, inspiring and funny. Then, as he was speaking, a fleeting thought zoomed through my mind: *I could do this! I could be a minister. I bet it would be fun!* So I embarked on my new journey armed with nothing more than an adult school course, an application to a state college and a vague dream of being called to a church.

I entered an innovative program that accepted some of my college credits from 20 years before. I went back to finish my bachelor's degree at night, and graduated on my 44th birthday—a mere 25 years after I'd started college! I then entered seminary at Union Theological in New York City, where I earned a Masters of Divinity. I was hoping to dovetail a part time parish ministry with my catering business. It seemed like a natural solution, a great way to have everything.

I was delusional, of course. During my internship at a local church, I realized that there's nothing part time about any ministry except for the salary. A minister can't turn off caring for the congregation; a minister never stops thinking about her role as a spiritual guide. And now, when almost every mainline church is seeing a decline in membership, ministers must often function on a salary that can't begin to cover the time and emotion they invest. It was increasingly difficult to accomplish my ministerial work while leaving enough time and energy to maintain the catering business in an increasingly competitive market. Although my partner insisted that the business needed both of us, I knew that for my own sanity I needed to fulfill the other aspects of my professional yearnings.

That fall, as I went online to register for a post graduate course at Fordham University, I discovered the Celebrant USA Foundation, which is an offshoot of an organization created and thriving in Australia. There was the answer to my dilemma, hiding in the middle of my web surfing. As I explored their website, I learned that Celebrant trains men and women to officiate at life's milestone moments: weddings, civil unions, funerals. Students learn the meaning and construction of ceremonies and rituals while being supported in building their own practices. *At last*, I thought. Here were all the aspects that I loved about ministry: interacting with people, researching myths and ceremonial elements, and the chance to perform inspiring ceremonies that truly reflected my clients' beliefs and values. And with none of the aspects I wasn't so keen about: why are the windows leaking? Who's going to shovel the snow to the church entrance? It was perfect! I could perform ceremonies part time while still enjoying some of the work and rewards of my catering business. In less time than it took to order jeans from the Gap, I was enrolled. Nine months later I graduated and was ordained. Three days after that, I performed my first wedding ceremony.

What started out as a part time lark turned into a thriving business. Couples were finding me, booking me, loving the ceremonies I'd learned to create. Then my world changed. My partner in the catering business—my ex-husband who was still my best friend—passed away suddenly. Soon after, our business was gently dismantled. As a buffer against insolvency I took a job as business development manager for a growing corporate catering company. I liked the company and the owner, and the growth potential within our market was rich. It seemed like the perfect fit: a job I could do for a company I liked and a reliable paycheck, something that many years of self-employment had never guaranteed.

> "It seemed like the perfect fit: a job I could do for a company I liked and a reliable paycheck. There was just one problem: I wasn't exactly a model employee."

There was just one problem: I wasn't exactly a model employee. Yes, I was a tireless worker. I was conscientious, happy to do whatever was needed to please our clients. But the concept of actually being *employed*, showing up at the same place, doing roughly the same thing (even something that I liked) was foreign territory for me. I began to wonder out loud how my friends with "real" jobs ever got anything else accomplished. When did they go to yoga class, or get the dog groomed or the car inspected? And, of course, when was I supposed to do some of the celebrant work I'd grown to love so much? But I hung in there, did my best and put my dreams aside—as I helped my boss' dreams come true.

Then there came a fateful day at the Jersey shore. A cloudless March sky formed the backdrop for a wedding ceremony I was to perform at 11:55 A.M. on a Tuesday. This was curious timing for a wedding ceremony. It was chosen by the bride's mother, who had consulted a combination of ancient Chinese astrology and numerology to come up with the date, time and place: March 15th, just before noon, southeast of Secaucus, New Jersey. I took the day off; I got up early, put on my black suit and drove down to the beach, Steely Dan blaring during the whole drive. We met near a deserted beachfront gazebo. The bride, dressed in a diaphanous white gown under a puffy down parka, looked like a small, misplaced marshmallow. The groom, tuxedoed and nervous, paced the parking lot. It was a peculiar setting for career magic to happen. But magic did happen as I realized, finally, that this was my true calling. I was euphoric as I contemplated life as a fulltime wedding officiant. As I drove home from the ceremony, I knew that I had to throw caution to the wind and quit my job; my last day would be my 51st birthday!

I'd already taken the first steps. I had engaged a talented design company to redesign my homemade website to make me stand out as a professional. Now, I started to attend business networking meetings and took marketing classes specifically for wedding professionals. I made sure that every ceremony I performed was uniquely crafted. I cultivated bridal coordinators and reception venues, and did everything I could to make it easy to find me. And my great couples helped too, providing testimonials and referrals that quickly grew my practice.

Almost three years later, I can joyfully say this is my full time career, and I feel so unexpectedly lucky; I approach every day with immense gratitude. I officiate at about 100 weddings and civil unions a year, along with baby blessings and adoption celebrations, end of life memorials and pet funerals. I even delivered the benediction before a mini marathon using a microphone plugged into a golf cart! I have met some of the most fascinating couples, heard the most heartwarming (and heartbreaking) stories, witnessed joy and sorrow beyond my wildest dreams. I've married people in wheat fields and in penthouses, in swamps and at museums. I consider myself very, very lucky to have found a calling that lets me write and perform, discover ancient rituals and invent new ones, and be part of the moments that change lives forever.

And I still travel with 200 feet of extension cord.

Celia Milton is a full time civil celebrant who creates innovative wedding and civil union ceremonies in New Jersey, New York and Pennsylvania.

Boiling the Frog

Lisa Doyle

If you drop a frog in a pot of boiling water, he'll hop right out and save himself. However, if you place a frog in a pot of cool water, turn on the burner and let the water heat up gradually, the frog will allow himself to be boiled to death. I think a lot of us have felt like the second frog at one time or another. I know that at my lowest I certainly did.

Right after graduating from college, I moved back to the Chicago suburbs to intern at a business-to-business magazine for executives in the cosmetics industry. They threw me in the deep end of the pool right away, and I was writing up to ten departments and three full-length features each month. It was a great opportunity, and I learned more in my first month there than I did in four years of college classes. At the end of the summer, I was hired full time.

The only downside to the company was its small size—after two years there, I was certain that the only way I could move up would be if someone above me quit or got fired. So when an assistant managing editor position opened up at a rival publishing house, I jumped at the opportunity.

I was surrounded by other like-minded young women in their mid-twenties; the hours were good, my paycheck 25% bigger than at my previous job, my cubicle much larger as well. This company, like my previous one, was family-run, and we were rewarded with generous bonuses, profit sharing and creative freedom. I was friendly with my

Lisa Doyle

colleagues and we even started a bowling league together. My husband was at school most nights, and I'd spend this time either with my bowling buddies or volunteering at a local resource center for low-income families. Everything was great.

Until the recession began. When magazine advertisers start hurting financially and cut back on their pages, the magazines, and thus the staffs, get smaller and smaller. When someone leaves, it isn't a chance to move up, but rather a chance to absorb someone else's workload. That's how it was for me. The bonuses became a distant memory. Office friendships fell apart as we become increasingly bitter toward one another. There was no more bowling. The pot was slowly working its way up to a simmer.

I'm not naïve, and I'm not trying to throw my former company under a cliché bus. I know that this was a pattern repeated in workplaces around the globe. But that didn't make it easier on anyone. You're wracked with survivor's guilt when you don't get laid off, and then you alternate between feeling grateful to have a job at all, and resentful because it's not the one you feel you deserve. Then, you're scared to lose your job and worried that your employer will take advantage of your fearful state. Rinse and repeat.

One night while surfing the jobs on Craigslist after a particularly long, snowy commute home, I thought I'd found my ticket out: a managing editor opening for the magazine of a locally-based organization. Huge pay increase? Fifteen-minute drive in the morning? Chance to head up a magazine my own way? Sign me up!

Soon after sending in my resume, they called me back, and I came in for an interview. The organization's president was like someone out of a movie—confident but congenial; a fair and trusted leader; a self-made millionaire by the age of forty. He explained his humble beginnings as a salesman, how he worked his way up to leading this organization while simultaneously running two other companies.

There was something else I noticed about him, that I'd never seen in anyone other than actors in commercials: he smiled as he spoke. He put me at ease, and I was positive I wanted to work for an amazing leader like him. He kept complimenting my portfolio, told me how impressed he was with me, and then put the ball in my court, asking me to call *him* if I was interested in pursuing the job. I called the very next day, met with him again less than a week later, and was promptly offered the job. The next thing I knew, I was gleefully skipping away from my previous employer. My husband was skeptical of the whole thing—this guy, the organization, the rapid hiring process, but I waved off his doubts. I felt like someone was finally recognizing my potential, and I didn't want him souring it for me.

The president, whom I soon found out was the direct boss of every employee at the company, wasn't there on my first day. My new coworkers on the magazine offered to take me out to lunch, and I gladly agreed. "Great," they said. "We'll leave at noon."

By 11:58, all were fidgeting in their seats, anxiously looking around and grabbing their coats. Two minutes later, we stampeded out of the office, rushed for the elevator, then power-walked to a nearby pub. We were promptly seated and my coworkers whipped a menu at me, drumming their fingers on the table and tapping their feet until a waiter arrived only seconds later to collect our orders. Puzzled, I asked, "Er, what's the rush?" Knowing looks were exchanged around the table. Later that day, I was informed that a few months back, someone had gotten fired on the spot for returning late from lunch. Yikes.

The boss returned to work the next day. I wasn't afraid of him, although my other coworkers seemed to be. After all, we had gelled so well in the interviews—I was almost surprised he didn't hug me at the end of each one! Undaunted, I bounced into his office.

"Good morning!" I brightly said.

He briefly looked up from his computer screen. "What do you need," he asked, more of a statement.

"Oh! Um. Just wanted to say hello… hope you had a nice vacation."

"It was fine." He continued to stare at his computer screen.

He shot me an irritated look and closed the door behind me as I scampered out.

One of my coworkers offered an explanation.

"The boss believes that people are only motivated by two things: greed and fear," he said. "So, to get you here, he tells you everything you want to hear. He'll say he thinks you're a genius, and he hints that you might get a huge bonus, and he says he gives out raises a few times a year. And then to *keep* you here, he just makes you constantly on edge and scared of being fired."

Over the next few weeks, I saw several people come and go—the turnover rate seemed to rival that of a fast-food joint, not a professional organization. Morale wasn't just low, but nonexistent. From what I could gather, most of my coworkers felt as duped as I did. One month in, I could only be certain of four things:

1. I had made a big mistake by taking this job (perhaps the hardest thing for me to admit at all).

2. I'd cheerfully burned my bridges with my last employer.

3. I'd had to quit volunteering—because of my strict work schedule, I couldn't make it to the resource center on time any longer.

4. Pot. Frog. Full boil.

Most mornings, I'd wake up well before my alarm, shaking, nervous, anxious about the day ahead and what the boss was going to say to me, or say to me without saying anything at all. I was suddenly afraid of other things that had never scared me before—driving on the highway (what if I crash?), flight turbulence (ditto), certain foods (what if I have an allergic reaction?). I lost about 15 pounds in six weeks. Some days I couldn't even eat my lunch. I was throwing up in the bathroom at work at least once per day. Sometimes my hands or feet would suddenly go numb. I've had occasional migraines all my life, but now a week didn't go by without one rendering me bedridden.

My husband, the rock in my life, even started to lose patience with this strange version of me, and I couldn't blame him. My doctor put a name to what I was experiencing—panic attacks—and recommended I see a psychologist. At the end of my first session, my therapist asked if there was any way I could afford to quit my job before finding a new one. I didn't think so. Part of me wanted to find a way get fired just to end the nightmare, but maybe the boss had the right idea after all—

fear *was* what made me mind my Ps and Qs. I was afraid of what getting canned would feel like, that I'd feel like a failure.

Trying to remain calm and appear normal started to feel like a fulltime job. I saw the therapist once a week, started listening to Belleruth Naparstek CDs every night and subliminal relaxation exercises on my iPod to get me through the day. I woke up before six each morning to play a stress abatement DVD, in which I'd focus on tensing focused areas of my body before relaxing them. All in all, when I wasn't feeling panicked, I was practically in a daze. I wasn't myself anymore, and I hated who I had become.

My husband urged me to get back into what made me feel good about myself—volunteering—but again, I didn't think I could get there on time with the strict work schedule. One day, I surfed around on the resource center's website to see if there was anything else I could do for them—maybe a food drive, volunteering on Saturdays, something like that. Hmmm. Job opportunities? Click. The posting for "Volunteer Coordinator" caught my eye. I scanned the list of requirements.

"Excellent verbal and written communication skills." I should hope so, being an editor.

"Acute attention to detail." Would you like me to tell you exactly what I wore last Tuesday? I can.

"Five years work experience in volunteer management." Crap. Not so much. I emailed them my resume anyway. The director of operations left me a voicemail less than an hour later.

After work, I called her back, heart pounding. We talked for about forty-five minutes about what the job entailed—recruiting volunteers, organizing food drives, working with businesses in the community to spread the word about the resource center and more. Plus, she explained so much I had never even known about the center in all my years of volunteering—I thought we just gave out food and clothes, but I didn't know that we had art classes, an English as Second Language program, job assistance, computer classes and more, providing free services to over 20,000 people every year. If I got the job, I'd be help-ing to manage over 800 volunteers. The whole time, I kept thinking, *Yes! Yes! Yes! I can totally do this!* Then, she brought up salary. The range she cited was less than I was making at my current job. And it was also less than I was making at my previous job. Sigh. I told her I was really sorry, but I didn't think I could afford the pay cut. She understood, and told me to call her back if I changed my mind.

I shuffled into the living room to give my husband the details. I started welling up as I told him that, despite it being the perfect job, it was a significant pay cut, so there was no way I could pursue it. He looked at me like I had three heads.

"Are you crazy? What the hell is wrong with you?"

"What do you mean, 'what's wrong with me?' It's like, five grand less than I was making at my last job."

"So what? It's not like you'd never get a raise. You might as well look into it. You love that place!"

It's funny, but until that moment, it had never occurred to me that one could, or should, *ever* take a lower-paying job. But he was absolutely right. I called the director of operations right back, and she scheduled me for an official interview the following week.

> "I kept thinking, Yes! Yes! Yes! I can totally do this! Then, she brought up salary..."

We met after work and talked for over three hours. She asked me some tough, revealing questions—how would I disci-pline a volunteer? Would I classify myself as a leader or a doer?—and I was as frank as I could be. We learned quite a bit about each other, and she asked me to come in the next week for a test of my computer skills. About a week after the test, which would put the GMAT to shame, she called me to offer me the position. With tears streaming down my face and a grin from ear to ear, I accepted.

The next day, I felt my anxiety rising as I drove in to work. I was still terrified of the reaction my boss would have when I resigned—would he scream at me and cause a scene? Tell me what a horrible, unprofessional excuse for a human being I was? He did neither, and the whole event took less than two minutes. He seemed relieved to be rid of me and said I could leave immediately, so I did. I was home by 9:30 A.M. and promptly fell asleep for the next nine hours.

I haven't had a single panic attack in the 16 months that I've been the resource center's volunteer coordinator. I'm so grateful for this job in ways large and small. First of all, accepting this job clearly rescued me from some pretty unbearable mental and physical problems; it probably saved my marriage; and it got me back to the center that I so loved. I can't even begin to explain what a relief it was to start a new job when I knew I already had a deep respect for the mission and the people there. However, I had no idea that I would absolutely fall in love with it.

Most people's jobs are, at the heart of it, all about making money, selling products, etc.—in essence, how much they can get. This center is all about how much we can *give*. In our last year, we filled nearly 30,000 grocery carts with food, distributed 73,000 articles of clothing, saved 228 families from becoming homeless, gave out more than 900 computers, found 111 clients new jobs—the list goes on and on. This feeling I get, going into work every day and knowing that my job is meaningful—there's nothing like it.

A big part of my job is processing the online volunteer applications, which come straight to my email. I love making the first phone call, helping them decide which program would be the best fit for them and getting them scheduled to start with us. Volunteering makes people happy, and by getting them set up to begin, I'm helping to make people happy—I feel such a sense of accomplishment every time! I enjoy nothing more than getting to share my passion and educate the newbies about the center, and teach them how they can contribute, too.

Plus, this job came with so many delights I never even expected. Pressure to spend money on expensive clothes or going out to lunch?

That's long gone. Worries about competitors? Please—we'd be delighted for more food pantries to open! Inflexible schedules? Some days I work late, some days I leave early, and every Wednesday, I volunteer as a youth mentor and lunch with a local fifth-grade girl at her elementary school.

Looking back, I know it wasn't until I had bottomed out that I realized I needed a change … and that I needed *to* change. My brief stint at the panic-inducing job ended up being one of the best decisions I ever made. Had I never worked there at all, I likely wouldn't have even considered switching careers to work in the nonprofit sector. So, maybe I didn't leave the publishing world because I suddenly felt the call of a life of service to others—but I think it's enough that now, I'm responding to that call every day.

Lisa Doyle is the volunteer coordinator for the People's Resource Center, located in Wheaton, Illinois and is actively involved with Metropolitan Family Services and the DuPage Association of Volunteer Administration. She lives in Chicago with her husband.

Spreading Good Fortune

Jennifer Jack

The Beginning

Let me introduce a 10-year old girl named Jennifer. I was a clever and adventurous girl who passed the time inventing, crafting, and annoying my brother. My family was never certain if I would spring out of bed as an Indian, comedian, or zoo keeper—whoever I was, each day was an exciting journey. I was dedicated to living life to the full. Fearlessly I took (still take) risks. On one day, I decided that our family's pet, Snoopy, needed a snazzy new haircut. Our entire neighborhood laughed at my horrible grooming skills, but Snoopy didn't laugh!

As I matured, so did my business skills, and by 12 I started my first business called "Jennifer Fantistics," a handcrafted bracelet corporation known for its customer service. Each order was carefully packaged with a handwritten note explaining the history of the company, a detailed invoice, a generous discount for new customers, and a lovely fortune. Business ideas continued to flow and I was excited to grow up, go to college, and someday have a real job and maybe even own my own business.

Tough times were no stranger to me, though. I struggled to find my identity (as most teens do), made some bad choices, and often learned the hard way. While I always found an outlet in art, I still longed for deeper meaning to life. Four years of college helped me learn intense focus and helped with goal setting, which led to an amazing job as a

Jennifer Jack

graphic designer. Within my first year, I was awarded the highest company honor and named employee of the year. I continued to improve as a designer and photographer, and within only four years was promoted to Senior Graphic Designer. Still, I longed for deeper meaning in life.

The Turning Point

Through a series of failed relationships, I realized that fulfillment would not come from men, work or myself. I felt lost, and through the advice of a co-worker was encouraged to pray for wisdom, because wisdom is the only thing God promises to give when we ask. A sucker for guarantees, I began to pray and ask God to show Himself, help me find purpose in life, and to experience a love greater than I felt.

It didn't take long for God to make good on his promise. He shared with me the secret to life and happiness. I joyfully moved forward and was ready to start living. Armed with the truth that life flows from God, and that God is love, I was gifted a faith I'd never felt before. I finally knew what unconditional love felt like and held onto His promises to never leave or hurt me. My once broken heart was rebuilt and began to overflow with love. I had a new purpose in life: to learn how to love others as Christ did.

Getting Cleaned Up: The Soap Making Starts

I worked in the corporate world for many years, but was ready for a change and longed for a different career, a lifestyle that fed my mind, body and spirit while also providing a way to connect with and help others. While lying in bed, praying and reading a book on soap making, the Lord spoke to a deep down place inside me. Through faith, I knew instantly that my love of design, photography, and handcrafted things was my calling. With 110% enthusiasm, I followed the plan that God had whispered. In Chattanooga, Tennessee, Good Fortune Soap was born. I studied soap making, natural ingredients and the natural products industry as a whole. The fearless mad scientist I knew as a child took over as I experimented by making hundreds of batches of soap, scent combinations, shapes, colors, and more. I strove to perfect the process night and day while working full-time as a graphic designer.

Good Fortune marked its first big open house in December, 2006. In just two days, I sold hundreds of bars of soap and gift sets. Further, two Chattanooga-based gift shops placed orders, purchasing Good Fortune's entire collection of scents and gift sets. This success prepared me for the next step: going full time with soap. Most people knew I was clever, but secretly thought I was crazy for "following a promise from God to make soap." I knew that by traditional standards it was a risk to quit my job, and I'd have to give up most luxuries, but the promise was real. Life was just beginning. Without hesitation, I took the plunge. I sold my house, quit my stable job and took Good Fortune all the way.

A Rest Stop

But first I had to take a sabbatical. The timing couldn't have been more perfect. My love of people had grown and my love of stuff was gone. Having given away most of my possessions, having just moved into my new one bedroom apartment, I left to go to South Africa for 10 days with a dear friend. Little did I know God planned to break my heart so I could love more deeply like Him while also giving me fuel for Good Fortune. I volunteered to minister and love children while in South Africa. Witnessing poverty, illness and homeless children crushed my heart. Unconditional love, compassion and generosity took on new meaning to me.

The beautiful people of Mamelodi were the sweetest, happiest and most loving people I'd ever met, yet had so little. After a few days of singing, hugging, and playing with the children, my creative business side began to surface. Why did God bring me here and what did He really want me to do? Was it to play with children or did God want more? Deciding to spend more quality spiritual time with the children, I grabbed a crayon and made a "free prayer" sign while my friend grabbed a desk and three chairs. We were amazed at what happened next. The free prayer booth grew longer than all of the games, painting, and activity lines. Without a plan, each child sat down one by one, with their backs turned from the crowd, waiting to be prayed over.

> "I began to ask God to show Himself, help me find purpose in life, and to experience a love greater than I felt. It didn't take long for God to make good."

I had no idea what huge problems burdened such tiny hearts. The memory of their precious tears and stone cold expressions as they told us to pray for their mommy and daddy still lingers. The children longed so deeply to be held, touched, heard and reassured that it was going to be okay. But even through their pain and confusion, God was alive in their hearts and no one could take that away. My problems paled in comparison to looking into the face of a suffering child. After all, I asked God to show me how to love like Jesus, and He'd just shown me. Joyfully, I wanted to know how to continue to love and inspire others to do the same.

Making it Real

Coming home, I needed to create a business plan that configured how Good Fortune was going to change the world. I didn't just want an amazing product that I could bank. I wanted products that embodied positive thinking and touched people's lives physically and spiritually. The healing ingredients, recyclable packaging, and charitable donations were marketed to spread the word about the spirit of the company.

Giving back is a concept that was built into the foundation of Good Fortune, in fact, that is where we got our name. From the moment God whispered His plan, He also asked me to bless others. Good Fortune supported several charities for the hungry, impoverished children, and hurting women, but nothing felt like a perfect fit. Unsettled by this, I again asked for wisdom, and again God spoke. Building a business, creating products, empowering women and loving others was God's plan all along. Soap for Hope sprang from this fertile soil.

Soap for Hope

Soap for Hope's goals are to inspire and empower disadvantaged girls by teaching life skills, entrepreneurship training, and offering hope for a college education. The love Christ has poured out inspires me to equip these girls with the location, tools, raw materials and educational resources needed to start a business of handcrafting natural soap and body care products to sell—this was exactly how I received the blessing. Good Fortune will buy back most of the products from the girls so they can start college savings plans, and have them sell the rest for their personal use. Through weekly mentoring and community involvement, I hope to build self-esteem, independence and motivation to succeed. Once the local pilot program is successful, international growth is expected, with those products imported and sold as fair trade. Soap for Hope wants to shed light on how many disadvantaged girls are exploited, isolated and unsupported while giving these girls a voice, allowing them to thrive, not just survive.

And Now...

Currently, Good Fortune fills a production studio and store front in Athens, Tennessee. The studio was once my grandfather's dairy barn, but is now open to the public. My mother and I worked side-by-side renovating the studio that has grown to include retail, wholesale, private label, e-commerce and eco-friendly do-it-yourself parties and classes. I am excited to continue to grow Good Fortune alongside Soap for Hope. I like to think of my products as seeds. Eventually Soap for Hope will grow, and young leaders will emerge. There are so many young girls out there just waiting for the opportunity to bloom into successful, happy women.

Jennifer Jack lives in Athens, Tennessee. She runs a booming natural body care business, and also recently started a ministry, Soap for Hope, aimed at teaching disadvantaged girls and women to start their own businesses.

PART THREE

Of Marriage and Motherhood

Meet My Uterus, Meet Me

Donella Martin Braddix

Until the discovery of my fibroid, I'd never known my uterus. Before that, my womanhood had been a source of blinding shame, rendering the possibility of making peace with it seemingly incomprehensible.

I remember going on a weekend spiritual retreat on an Indian reservation in upstate New York with my aunt and cousin. I was pretty miserable during the retreat, turned off by the rustic surroundings and unable to feel a connection to any of the activities I had fantasized would change my life. During one women's prayer circle, the elder priestess entered a trance and asked all of the women who had suffered abortions or miscarriages to come forth and receive healing. Several women came forward. Standing next to my relatives, I was too ashamed to admit the sordid history of my uterus.

The woman, inspired by the revelations of her ancestors, opened her eyes and looked directly at me.

"You!" she said, beckoning me forward.

I meekly followed on numb legs. Blurrily, I could see my aunt and others following, but all I could think about was that she had exposed my shame for all to see.

All my life, I have been haunted by my mother's bitterly reluctant womanhood. I was tormented by the pleas of a frightened woman-child who, by giving birth at sixteen, had surrendered her girlhood way

Donella Martin Braddix

too soon. *Don't make the same mistakes I made,* she begged. I embodied her regrets, her frustrations, until I became her. Detached from the possibilities of my own present and future, I was the perpetual walking past. My life was hers, the sequel—the way it should have ended.

My uterus had betrayed me with its fertile usefulness, housing unwanted intruders with the propensity to crush my dreams and enslave me to a life of burdened servitude. It had been the site of massacres, bathing the blood of fetuses that would never see the light of the world; each month it became the epicenter of torturous pain for which I overdosed on ibuprofen in order to forget. I didn't want to know my uterus. It was a tragic inconvenience of my existence.

Now, here, it was speaking to me. By way of this fibrous growth, calling out, "I'm here!"

And suddenly, I felt a surge of possessiveness towards it. How dare this fibroid, this intruder come in and mar the surface of my uterus? I didn't ask for it. It had no right to be here. I began to suspect my uterus' magnificence, its uniqueness. I realized I must own it. And finally, I yearned to love it.

I began to imagine there was no greater expression of healing than to allow my uterus to embody its destiny. There was nothing that could reunite us, my uterus and me, as honestly and thoroughly as witnessing it actualize its true nature by nurturing a child.

At once, I realized my biological purpose. It was simple, unlike the grandiose fantasies that I'd nursed of being extra special, a pious role model leading humanity, of having fame and fortune. No, this humble role was absolutely simple and yet indescribably holy. I was meant to give birth.

> "I began to imagine there was no greater expression of healing than to allow my uterus to embody its destiny."

My body had transcended the mundane ordinariness of mere tissue, of cytoplasm-filled cells. It was now a vehicle employed by Heaven. I couldn't simply view my nakedness without imagining my breasts engorged with life-nurturing milk and the pursed lips of a child suckling them. I couldn't see my belly, appreciating the sexual allure of its softened curves, without feeling slightly disappointed that it wasn't rounded with a baby. I envied the pregnant women I saw in the supermarkets, in the restaurants and the apparent simplicity with which they endured their situations—a situation that, for me, had once seemed as miraculously improbable as walking the rings of Saturn.

But the envy was softened by wondrous pride. I was proud of having transcended the twisted lessons of my mother's past, which didn't belong to me. I was finally making my own rules. That I actually yearned for the privilege of bringing forth a new soul to this realm, instead of viewing it as an inconvenient mistake or a tolerable glitch signified my own glorious rebirth.

That a fibroid should have inspired such female possessiveness might be simply an example of human greed. But the phenomenon of breaking through the whispers of the past to finally introduce myself to my uterus, my womanhood and ultimately, myself, is nothing short of a miracle.

Donella Martin Braddix was born and raised in Brooklyn, New York. She spent many years teaching English in the public school systems of New York and Cleveland, Ohio. She has also lived in Japan and traveled extensively throughout Asia. She now finds herself comfortably ensconced in the desert of Arizona.

From "Mom" to "Me"

Mary Potter Kenyon

"It's totally up to you," the surgeon said. "If you're in pain and don't feel comfortable going home, then you should stay here overnight. It's better to stay than to come back at two in the morning."

I hadn't expected to stay in the hospital overnight. I didn't bring any toiletries with me, no comb, deodorant or even a toothbrush. But I was experiencing intense pain—from my gallbladder removal and the repair of a hernia near my navel, as well as crushing pain in my chest as the anesthesia wore off. The doctor sensed my indecision about the overnight stay.

"You don't have to decide now. See how you feel in a couple of hours and I'll be back to check on you. We can admit you later if you'd like."

I remembered how, after a previous surgery, I'd been raring to get home. I couldn't even imagine staying in the hospital overnight when there was a blonde-haired, brown-eyed toddler waiting to be nursed to sleep and who spent most of her nights sleeping curled next to me. But now I hesitated. I knew I was needed at home, but part of me wanted to stay here.

I thought back on what led me to this moment of uncharacteristic temptation to stay put for the night. How had I become the militant, extended breastfeeding, sleep-sharing attachment-style mother who refused to be away from her children? I was a college student when I

Mary Potter Kenyon

breastfed my first two children. I used to lie down with them for much-needed naps, but they both slept in a crib at night and weaned on their own, one at nine months, the other on her first birthday.

Our third baby, however, was a mother's nightmare, literally. By day, his temperament and personality were nearly beatific. He was an extremely happy baby, always smiling. His whole body shook with laughter at his sibling's antics. He rarely even cried. For the first few months I'd thought I'd hit the baby jackpot. Then, when he started teething around four months of age, sweet little baby Michael transformed into a nighttime monster. I could expect him to sleep for maybe two hours tops after his evening feeding, and then the nighttime Olympics would begin. Michael tossed and turned, crying out as if in pain, then screaming inconsolably until I lifted him out of his crib. I tried everything, but only rocking him in a rocking chair or dancing around the room with him in my arms worked to calm him. Good sleep usually eluded me until 5:00 A.M. when my husband David got up for work and took over. The nightmare lasted for a good twelve months.

Gradually and almost imperceptibly, I morphed into the die-hard attachment-style parent that completely puts her children first, the woman who doesn't bat an eye when her husband moves out of her bed and onto a mattress on the floor to make room for the children. After Rachel was born I didn't even bother with a crib; she started out sleeping in our bed, as did the rest of our children, who nursed with us in bed past their second birthdays. By the time baby number five had arrived I'd begun home schooling, too, ensuring long days caring for children without the break most mothers get.

Despite my small income from part time writing, we were mostly a one-income family, and the tight budget didn't allow for many indulgences. I cut my own hair. I became a coupon queen and frequented thrift stores and garage sales for our family's clothing. My own wardrobe consisted mostly of loose nursing tops and leggings or jeans. At one point I was invited to do a reading at a local bookstore from an anthology in which one of my pieces had been published. After checking my closet, I had to turn the opportunity down flat because I didn't have anything to wear.

Our move to a 100 year-old farmhouse in the country pounded the last nail into my coffin of isolation. The kids and I had full days of reading, writing and massive art projects, but we could go for days at a time without seeing anyone but our mailman. Sometimes I spent several days in a row wearing sweatpants and baggy sweatshirts, the highlight of my week a trip to the grocery store, when I "dressed up" in jeans and a cardigan.

Then, in the summer of 2006, David was diagnosed with cancer. Suddenly I was faced with the dilemma of having to leave my young children for hours each day so that I could be with him for the long days of chemotherapy and radiation treatments. Much to my surprise, my children not only survived, they thrived under their loving aunts' care. Three year-old Abby reveled in the hours of story time from my kind-hearted sisters. The older children pitched in on household chores and learned a few basic recipes for cooking food for their siblings.

> "I had morphed into the die-hard attachment-style parent that completely puts her children first, who doesn't bat an eye when her husband moves out of her bed to make room for the children."

At the onset of David's cancer, well-meaning friends urged me to take care of myself so I could take care of him. I was irritated by their suggestions to "take a walk," or "make sure you get time to yourself." I couldn't do that before David's diagnosis because of caring for young children; how could I do so afterward? As soon as I got home from the hospital each day, my children followed me around like parentless waifs as I struggled to keep up with the household chores that seemed overwhelming. I shrugged off the well-meaning advice.

Then something very unexpected happened. Though caring for my husband was time-consuming and difficult, it brought us closer together. It gave me a focus outside the children. It stripped years of habit away and exposed the deep feelings we had for each other. I started caring more about how I looked for my new-found love. After he came home from the hospital, David reclaimed his rightful place next to me in bed, where I listened for his breathing and reached out to him several times a night.

When he recovered sufficiently, David returned to work. About the same time, I weaned Abby, and the combination of the hormonal imbalance and the loss of the caregiver title suddenly left me distraught and anxious. I got up earlier and earlier to give myself a chance to be alone, but then crashed in an exhausted frenzy by nightfall. The children took the brunt of my frustration, with me snapping at them over the slightest infractions.

With David's encouragement, I joined a women's gym and start exercising, a luxury I would never have considered before. I started driving into town three mornings a week. As I toned up, my confidence and energy soared. Now when I got up early, it was to write in my journal for two hours, then go into town for my workout. I'd come home to help the children with schoolwork energized by the time alone and regular exercise. I lost some weight and my clothes fit better. After years of caring for the children and then David, I was finally learning to take care of myself.

We moved into town, within walking distance of a park, the library, and three of our four adult children. And, walk I did—at first just a mile, working my way up to two miles, then three, then five. I joined the local TOPS club (Take Off Pounds Sensibly) and between their support and the walking and biking, I lost more weight. That summer I prepared for a niece's wedding by shopping for a brand new dress, something I hadn't done for a long, long time. For the first time in years, I got a professional haircut.

Now my relationship feels new and exciting. I feel closer to my husband than ever before in our 29 years of marriage. Even more exciting is the way I feel about myself. Taking a walk or bike ride, I catch myself smiling, harboring an unaccustomed feeling I can only describe as contentment. I realize I am a much happier person and a better mother for learning to take care of myself. I feel younger and more vibrant than the isolated mom-at-home I used to be.

Truly, I am not the person I became during those difficult times. That's why, after my gallbladder surgery, I had that moment of indecision about staying overnight in the hospital. The old Mary wouldn't have hesitated. She would have thought about the children at home and worried more about them than her own needs. But the new Mary did more than consider an overnight stay. In fact, part of my indecision was that I secretly relished the idea. I may not have brought toiletries, but I'd brought two important things, a paperback book and my notebook. That was all I needed to treat the unexpected quiet time as a sort of retreat. So I settled in and enjoyed a night to myself, which I can now admit I so richly deserved.

Mary Potter Kenyon graduated from the University of Northern Iowa with a Bachelor of Arts degree in psychology. Her writing has been featured in *Home Education*, *The Sun*, *Our Iowa*, *Backwoods Home*, and *Woman's World* and she has essays in the books *Chicken Soup for the Soul*, *Homeschool Open House*, and *Voices of Caregiving*. Her book *Homeschooling from Scratch* was published in 1996. She lives with her husband David and four of her eight children in Manchester, Iowa.

Finding My Corner of the Sky

Camille Ehrenberg

"Life is a journey, not a destination," so the saying goes. But I only partially buy into this saying. I am not so goal-oriented that I fail to appreciate the scenery of my everyday existence, but I am the type of person who always has a destination entered into my internal GPS. That said, often, after I've arrived at my destination, pitched my tent and gotten the lay of the land, I've decided that I need to move on. In fact, I have done this quite a few times. I'm not sure what this behavior reveals about me. A mercurial nature? Rashness? Adventurousness? I'd like to think that I am on a journey to find my place in the world, where I can be true to myself and in some small way work towards making the world a better place. I consider myself extraordinarily lucky to have been able to explore the possibilities, to have opened and passed through many doors.

It was my luck to be born in the United States, into a middle class family and to have devoted parents. Both of my parents were the children of immigrants. Their childhoods were difficult, especially my father's. He took parenting extremely seriously; he often said, "I have a duty to myself, to God and this country to shape you into a responsible and honorable woman." Yep, my dad was a serious guy. For 10 years, I spent an hour and a half each Monday evening in a car with my father traveling to and from piano lessons. I was a captive audience, and he used this opportunity to share his life philosophy. (My mother and I referred to these talks as "indoctrination.") Sadly, I am not much of a

Camille Ehrenberg

pianist, but in retrospect it was worth practicing the piano just to spend time with such an insightful human being. "Do something meaningful with your life, and you will never dread getting out of bed each morning to go to work," was one of his many lessons. Another was, "You have an obligation to leave the world a little bit better than when you entered it." These conversations played a large part in shaping me, and later fueled my search for my perfect career.

My Science Experiment

I always loved science, particularly biology. When I was a little girl, my father brought home a used high school biology text that he picked up at the secondhand bookshop he frequented. I would sit on the living room sofa and pore over the photos and diagrams. I couldn't read yet, but the photo of a mother and son who could shape their tongues into a cloverleaf was interesting even with an indecipherable caption. Years later, when I arrived at the State University of New York at Albany, I and fell in love with cellular biology.

Cells are a microcosm of multicellular animals like you and me. They grow and move; they need oxygen. They obtain nutrients and metabolize them. They reproduce and die. They are complex and beautiful. And so I decided to make my life's work studying cellular processes, and particularly what happens when things go awry. During my senior year, I worked in a lab in the Biological Sciences department. Among other things, I was part of a team whose work led to the publication of a journal article in *Cell*, an MIT scientific journal. It was entitled *Human fibroblast-conditioned medium contains a 100K Dalton glucose-regulated cell surface protein*. I know—I can hardly believe it either. During this year, I also applied to the Ph.D. programs at Harvard, Yale and Columbia. My first choice was Harvard because at the time, there were labs studying interferon, proteins that inhibit viral replication, and there was hope that interferon might be the magic bullet in the fight against cancer. My acceptance letter arrived in April.

However, after graduation, I began having doubts about whether I wanted to spend my life working in a lab. Devoting one's life to the battle against cancer was surely one way to make the world a better place. Yet, I knew that it was not my calling. In July, after traveling to Boston to find housing, I could no longer ignore my inner voice urging me to get back on the highway and take another exit. I called Harvard, withdrew from the program, and began to contemplate what to do next.

Attorney

After working for a year as a paralegal at a large Wall Street firm, I decided to give the law a try. I know—lawyers might not be on many

Top 10 lists of humanitarians, but despite popular opinion, being a lawyer and making a positive contribution to society are not mutually exclusive.

Upon arriving at New York University School of Law, I realized that I had journeyed to a foreign country. I had to learn a totally different way of thinking. Scientists ask a question, construct a hypothesis, conduct an experiment and learn whether or not their hypothesis is true. Lawyers start by identifying the desired result, and then construct an argument to get there. It is very much like playing chess; you are bound by an established set of rules, but within those bounds, you're limited only by your own ingenuity, creativity and ethics.

> "I had a love/hate relationship with my job. I loved helping my clients; I hated who I had to be each day."

After my second year of law school, I was hired as a summer associate at a mid-sized Manhattan law firm. In addition to the usual specialties—litigation, corporate law, tax and trust and estates—the firm specialized in libel law, and that is what caught my attention. Defending a newspaper's First Amendment right to free speech was a positive contribution to the world, right? At the end of the summer, I received an offer to work at the firm upon graduation. Thus began my eight-year stint as a litigator.

I practiced general and libel litigation for about 3 years. Then, after an associate in the Matrimonial Department left the firm, I was asked to pinch-hit and write a brief in a custody dispute. For a while, I split my time between libel and matrimonial cases, but when I was asked to choose a department, I chose matrimonial law. The personal aspect of this work was very appealing. I was no longer representing a corporation; I was representing a human being who was in pain. Some of my clients were eager to start a new life. Others were angry and/or scared about the termination of their marriage. It was my job to help smooth the transition and to ensure that their future was secure. It was grueling but satisfying work.

During my five years as a matrimonial attorney, I had a view of human beings who were not always on their best behavior. It was hard to believe that husband and wife, now plaintiff or defendant, had ever agreed to spend an hour together, let alone a lifetime. Without a doubt, the lowest point was the alleged murder of one of our clients by his wife. She went to his studio apartment with a knife from the kitchen of her Park Avenue apartment and stabbed him in the back. After two days of deliberations, the jury failed to convict her. One juror noted that they did not believe her, but they did not have the evidence to convict her beyond a reasonable doubt. I still have not gotten over this tragedy.

There was another aspect to my job that over time became difficult for me: the constant arguing. Every morning I had to check my true personality at the door of the law firm and don a pair of boxing gloves. I realized that I had a love/hate relationship with my job. I loved helping my clients through rough periods in their lives; I hated who I had to be each day and the shenanigans in the Matrimonial Bar.

Motherhood

Some women know that they want to be mothers from the moment they hold their first doll. I am not one of them. However, when my father died I paused to assess where my life was ultimately headed. I knew that when the time came for me to draw my last breath and my life flashed before my eyes, I wanted to see more than summonses, complaints, motions and briefs. Being blessed with two daughters resolved my dilemma. What a privilege to nurture a child and guide her into the adult world; what a delight to experience the world anew through the eyes of a child.

When my first daughter was born, I got a six-month respite from the law. I planned to go back on a four day per week basis. But by the end of three months, I knew that it would be impossible for me to return.

On a good day, I arrived home from work at eight, and my husband, also a lawyer, arrived home well after that. When would our baby see her parents? Why did we have this child, if only to hand her off to someone else to raise her? Yet, I also thought of the many women who came before me and fought for the right of future generations of women to have a seat in a law school class. Was I betraying them and undermining the process for other women if I stopped practicing law to become a mommy? And what message was I sending the law firm? That training and investing in a female associate was risky business because ultimately they would leave? My husband and I discussed the situation, and after a lot of thought, I resigned my position at the law firm and took on the job of a full time mother.

I am my father's daughter, and I learned early on that parenting is a serious matter, a "duty." He also taught me that anything worth doing was worth doing well. I began to read and study parenting books. I wanted to learn more about child development. So for fun I took a course in child development at Bank Street College, Graduate School of Education, and was hooked. I began to think about teaching.

When my second daughter was two years old, the director of the Parenting Center at the 92nd Street Y approached me about joining their staff. From infanthood, both of my children had taken the many wonderful classes offered by the Parenting Center, and I had gotten to know the teachers of those classes quite well. One of them, privy to my long-range plan to teach one day, suggested to the director of the Parenting Center that I would make a wonderful group leader. I was thrilled to have this opportunity.

Ultimately, I was able to pursue a graduate degree in education at Bank Street. My younger daughter, then four years old, was in nursery school and my older daughter was a third grader at The Dalton School. I'd spent years as a scientist and as a lawyer, but once I entered the classroom as part of my fieldwork requirement, I knew that I had finally found not only my passion, but my calling.

Teacher

It was motherhood that led to my career in teaching, and it was my children who led me to a position at The Dalton School. As my younger daughter entered kindergarten and my older daughter began 4th grade at Dalton, I joined the Dalton faculty as an Associate Teacher. This summer, I will have completed my ninth year as a First Grade Head Teacher at Dalton.

I love my job. Teaching, like parenting, is rewarding and challenging. It's a privilege to be part of the lives of 18 children and their families each year. It's thrilling to watch each child grow socially, emotionally and intellectually. It is also exciting to work with, learn from and teach the young associate teachers that work with me. It is a gift to work in a school with supportive colleagues, where students and faculty can follow their passions, where creativity and intellectual pursuit are nurtured.

As a teacher, I obviously want my students to become better readers, writers and mathematicians over the course of first grade, but I also want them to become better people. I believe that it is my "duty" to help cultivate in them respect, integrity, compassion, a sense of justice and an understanding of their future roles as stewards of the planet. "Your job, I tell my students, "is to help make the world a better place." These are the lessons that I hope my students take with them and carry in their hearts. I have planted seeds that I hope family, friends and other teachers will nurture.

So, the last decade of my journey through life has been in the classroom. My life as a teacher is fulfilling; I certainly never dread getting up in the morning to go to work, and I believe that my work in the classroom will leave this world a little bit better than when I entered it. I've pitched my tent. I like the view. Right now, I plan to stay.

Camille Ehrenberg lives in New York, New York with her husband, two daughters and kitty. She teaches first grade at The Dalton School.

My Elephant Child Life

Mary Lynne Hill, Ph.D.

While serving as a tenured professor at my alma mater, at the tender young age of 41, I gave birth to my son, AJ, a petite bruiser of ten pounds, two ounces. Prior to AJ's birth, I had earned a Ph.D. I loved being "Dr. Hill," a college professor, particularly at *my* school (where I had met and married my husband, Andy). I loved teaching and meeting with my students; I loved my son. Unfortunately, I had no idea how to balance the demands of these great loves. Balance and boundaries are not my strong suit; I tend to plunge head first into whatever has my attention and not come up for air until the situation is untenable.

While home on maternity leave, I had the chance to be quiet with my wonderful child. I had never before been so quiet for such a long period in my life. The contrast between my life's internal and external noise levels pre-AJ and post-AJ was stark, and it prompted within me a profound introspection. During those months, my mind and heart would alternate between the peaceful, utter stillness of a mill pond and the unnerving shrill of the Mommy War Harpies shrieking opposing messages: "Go back to work, or you're a professional loser" versus "Stay at home with your child, or you don't really love him!" I had tenure, for crying out loud. No one quits an academic job once they've survived the hazing process of tenure. I had to hush those voices if I were to fight my way to a reconciliation of my professional and familial lives.

Photo: Marian Hill

Mary Lynne Hill, Ph.D.

I knew that I could not go back to my school work until AJ was ready to tackle his own. I often wondered how my own mother felt about leaving my siblings and me to go back to work, especially because so few women in her generation had a professional career like she did. Maybe she understood that I would be okay if she continued her career. Maybe she was better at boundaries than her daughter.

Boundaries have been difficult for me to build and maintain, because so much of my life has worked well without them. But such permeability can be a dangerous thing. Colleagues, bosses, students wear you out, leaving you vulnerable. Then, something as fantastic as a child bursts into your life, and you can quickly become overwhelmed. My reason for being cannot solely be my son. That is too much of a burden for any child to bear.

So I have been learning how to reconcile my old life with my new life that was born the day I had AJ. To prevent the Harpies from crippling my present by shrieking about my beloved past, I've had to get innovative in nurturing my new life. One way of doing this has been working with the form of a wonderful image: Ganesha, the Elephant Child. Not too long ago, I found myself reading Joan Chittister's *Welcome to the Wisdom of the World: and Its Meaning for You*. In it, she retells the Hindu story of Shiva, the mighty god of destruction and joy, and his beautiful wife, Parvati. It is a story of picking up the pieces to create something new.

Shiva and Parvati lived happily in the mountains. Being such an important god, Shiva was often on the road, destroying and rebuilding, often for years at a time. During one of these lengthy business trips, Parvati grew quite lonely. However, before she despaired, she was inspired.

"I will create a child!"

With clay and water, Parvati molded a beautiful round little boy. Even as she worked the clay to form his chubby legs, she was already beginning to love him. When she had finished, she laid the child in the sun, and he warmed to life under its fiery gaze.

Parvati was thrilled and over the next few years, her chubby, cheerful playmate soothed her loneliness. One warm day, while they were out walking, Parvati told her son she was going to bathe in a stream to cool down. "Guard the path to the stream" she told him. "Do not let anyone pass." The boy soldier took his post quite seriously. Not too long had passed before the mighty Shiva appeared on the path. Drawing himself up to his full height, the boy cried out, "Stop. You may go no further."

Shiva smiled at the cherubic child, trying to brush him aside. But the boy was tenacious, determined to block the god's path. In his annoyance, Shiva pulled out his sword and cut off the boy's head.

Parvati, who had heard the scuffle, was already racing up the path, crying out in anguish at the scene in front of her. Shiva did not understand.

"You have slain our son!" she gasped, collapsing on the ground next to the boy's body.

Shiva was shocked. "But we have no children," he cried in bewilderment. Parvati sobbed, "I was lonely with you gone for such a long time, so I created our son."

The god held his head in his powerful hands, trying to comprehend what he had just done. Parvati looked up at her husband.

"You must go into the forest and bring back the head of the first creature you see. Then, you will affix it to our child's body and breathe new life into him."

Shiva, desperate to ease Parvati's suffering, crashed through the forest with his bloodied sword, stopping suddenly when confronted by the first creature in his path, a young elephant. He gazed at the wonderful creature, blessing the animal for its sacrifice, as he was simultaneously condemning his own actions.

Returning to Parvati, he affixed the elephant's head to the body, silently fearing his wife's response to this mutant being as he breathed new life into it. Stepping back, he smiled in relief, as Parvati began to stroke the newborn child's trunk until he laughed. She was delighted, thinking that this new child, Ganesha, was perhaps even more loveable than the first one. Shiva, also, found himself quickly falling in love with the boy, wondering in this new creation.

As a Midwesterner-turned-Texan-Catholic, I was unnerved by this story the first time I read it. It seemed so foreign, until I began to recognize such radical reconstructive surgery in and of my own life. Except I, myself, had slain my old life. After much fear and trembling and in a much less dramatic stroke than Shiva's, I had severed my tie with my old life with the stroke of a pen, abandoning the security of tenure for the unknown with my husband and child.

With the stroke of this pen, however, I did not magically stop being a professional woman and morph into June Cleaver. It has been much messier than that, much more painful, and much more fiscally disastrous. Much more wobbly—like a child with an elephant head on a little fat body, disorienting and unsettling. But I've tried to bear the consequences of my choice like Parvati. Parvati remained open to a new source of joy and received Ganesha for her trust in the goodness of life itself. Learning from Parvati's openness, I have been slowly reconciling my two great loves of education and family, stitching them together into a new elephant/child life.

This image of Shiva and Parvati adapting to their circumstances, working things out with what was available to them, has helped me to shape my new professional-familial life. No, I don't have contact with students every day any more, but I can still work on my own research and writing. No, I no longer have a clear identity as Dr. Hill, but I've had the opportunity to develop a political aspect of my identity in ways that I never have before, currently serving as a precinct chair and an election judge with people who only know me as Mary Lynne. And, I have had the rich opportunity to develop the maternal aspect of my identity with someone who only knows me as Mama. With each passing day, I try to nurture the life-growing possibilities of my emerging elephant child life. I am not sure what my

> "After much fear and trembling, I had severed my tie with my old life with the stroke of a pen, abandoning the security of tenure for the unknown with my husband and child."

Ganesha will look like in the next five years, but in the present, I know that I am profoundly grateful for having had the chance to reconcile my old life as a professional woman and wife, with my new life as a professional woman, wife, and mother—the chance to play Shiva by breathing new life into an old one.

Mary Lynne Hill lives with her husband, Andy, and her son, AJ, on a family farm in Texas. She is currently an independent scholar, writer, and civic engagement consultant. She has recently finished co-editing a Civil War diary, *The Uncompromising Diary of Sallie McNeill, 1858-1867*, with Ginny McNeill Raska, which will be released by Texas A&M Press.

Being a Wife Is Not Enough
Bobbi Leder

It wasn't easy making the decision to give up my career to follow my husband as he pursued his to points overseas. I became what I had always loathed: a trailing spouse. I lost all respect for myself and worse yet, others lost respect for me as well. "I have a degree from Rutgers University," I would say, but they just stared at me with glazed eyes as if I had told them I was capable of wiping my bum all by myself. I filled my days with baking, cooking gourmet meals, cleaning, handling all of the financial and administrative duties and exercising.

As I went through these stifling routines day after day, I found myself longing more and more desperately for a career of my own. I craved the self worth I had once felt, and wondered why I had taken a giant step backwards when I was such a feminist at heart. I just knew Gloria Steinem was shaking her head in disgust. I was glad when my husband's career gained momentum, but at what cost? I felt dead inside and had lost all sense of myself.

Finally, when I could no longer stand to look at myself in the mirror, I gave my husband an ultimatum: either we move back to the States where I could have stability and a career, or we go our separate ways. He called my bluff. We moved to Houston, Texas a few months later.

But getting that career going was harder than I'd thought it would be. Having moved for my husband 12 times in 13 years, and bouncing around from town to town, state to state, and country to country, I wasn't exactly an employer's dream candidate. I applied for just about anything, since beggars can't be choosers, but the obvious was staring me in the face—and I was even told point blank – that no one would hire me. I was too much of a flight risk, and I had no recent references since I had been living in the United Kingdom for six years, and in three different locations there.

So out of frustration I started to write; after all, I did have a degree in journalism. This move shouldn't have come as a surprise to anyone, but for some reason it did. I guess my family was amazed that I was actually doing something for myself instead of for my spouse. That's how completely I'd given up my identity. One writing job led to another, and then another, and before I knew it, I was actually working full time as a freelance writer. And the best part was the fact that I was earning money. Okay, it wasn't much money, but it was my money.

> "I was glad when my husband's career gained momentum, but at what cost? I felt dead inside and had lost all sense of myself."

Knowing we were going to have stability for a long time to come, I made another life changing decision, to adopt a dog. And not just any dog, but a high maintenance English Cocker Spaniel named Euri. Suddenly my life revolved around Euri and my job, so I had little time for my husband. I became the Houston Dogs Examiner and because of my passion for animals, a new woman blossomed inside of me; a woman that was passionate about her life again.

Whenever I felt guilty about not giving my husband all of my attention or cooking him a five course meal, I reminded myself that I had paid my dues being "the wife." It was only fair that I had an opportunity to feel proud of my accomplishments as well. Knowing I made a difference in the lives of both animals and people was (and still is) a satisfying feeling, one that changed me for the better. I finally found what was missing all of those years as a trailing spouse: my true calling, and myself.

Now I feel like I am an equal partner in my marriage, which is a much healthier place than where I used to be. I am no longer "the wife;" I am my own person with my very own career. Ms. Steinem would be proud.

_____

Bobbi Leder is a freelance writer living in Houston, Texas with her husband and cocker puppy, Euri. She has been published in magazines and on many websites. Bobbi is an Opinion writer for a Houston paper and serves as the the City of Houston Dogs Examiner.

The Goddess Within

Shadiyah

The lights go down. The music swells: sitars, *ouds*, finger cymbals, the drums of North Africa, a sound as rich and colorful as the traditions they herald. I wait in the dark behind a curtain, making quick, last second adjustments to my traditional two piece belly dancing costume that blazes with gems, crystals and beading that will catch the stage lighting and echo the notes of the instruments as I express the melodies, rhythms and sounds with the movements of my body. I close my eyes and whisper a prayer, summoning my innermost spirit so I may share my gifts to connect with the souls in the audience.

My imagination transports me back in time. I'm a child again, waiting in the dark—a little American Catholic girl of Italian descent sitting in the rec room as my father flips on the projector to show us movies of his adventures to exotic places like Egypt and Turkey. It's Christmas time. The room is decorated just so. My two older sisters and I have just sung our favorite carols and I did a special dance I made up just for the occasion. Most children love to play games; I love to dance and sing. I can get lost in moving my little body to any rhythm man or nature can create. Today, I'm so happy that Daddy is back that I danced myself dizzy.

There's snow outside, a child's greeting card playground, but my eyes are riveted to the screen. From my earliest days, I am captivated by the world's different cultures. I feel there is a common, sacred thread that

Shadiyah

ties us all together in spite of many apparent differences. My sisters and my mother watch with me, eyes riveted to the screen as Daddy brings the scenes to life with vivid descriptions of his travels. My sisters and I don't know it yet, and maybe my mother doesn't either, but a divorce will carry him away from us again, never to return to the safety of our nuclear family.

But now, as he talks of the beautiful Nile, the pyramids, the sands of Egypt—the same sand, perhaps, that once softened the footfalls of the people who animate my Sunday school lessons—I think only of the amazing images. I sit with my family, happily unaware that this home will one day be broken, and imagine the scene repeated in some fantastic future, a future in which I am the wife and mother. A future where the holiday hearth is decorated with goodies for my children. Where my husband shows Granddaddy's home movies to *our* children.

Years later, I am feeding my body with work in retail and my soul by singing at church. My oldest sister has started having children and I'm eager to follow in those footsteps. But there's time for that. I'm young, vibrant, talented, attractive and have a bright future.

The future rolls on, year by year. Retail is a dead end with no challenges, and I find myself in the gray flannel world of defense contracting for several years, then the life insurance and estate planning business. Insurance is a solid business with a solid future, which means a great deal to me since the uncertain days following my parents' divorce. After all, we're expected to be responsible; my conservative upbringing constantly reminds me of the "duties" I'm supposed to fulfill. I'm still confident that the right man, the father of my children and my mother's grandchildren, is out there. It's hard sometimes, though. My middle sister has just found out she's unable to bear children. I feel dreadful for her, and I know Mom is upset too. Upset not only for her daughter, but for the grandchildren she'll never hold. Until I bear more of them, that is. The expectation to produce the next generation falls heavier on me. More pressure.

> "Letting go of the need to define myself as a mother has been incredibly liberating. It's better to just be me."

All that stuff I hear about the biological clock ticking turns out to be true. It keeps me awake some nights, it ticks so loudly. When I'm at church, gently smiled on by images of the Madonna and Child, I can't help but look at the mothers and their beautiful children sitting in the pews. I raise my voice to God and catch myself wishing the hymn book were a baby. *My* baby. I feel guilty. My sister's plight increases not only my longing for a child, but a sense of obligation that grows each day. Since my earliest days, I've looked ahead to Motherhood Day with eagerness and joy. Now it's starting to feel like an imaginary cliff, with the biological clock behind me pushing, pushing.

I can still lose myself in dance, though. The home movies of my childhood are still vivid as I study the cultures of the world and absorb the traditions of dance that have given women a special mode of expression for thousands of years. Generation after generation, in culture after culture, dance has been a way for women, especially oppressed women, to express and share their joys and frustrations, triumphs and heartaches. Women have seldom had an equal voice, and sometimes it feels like I don't, either, as I navigate through a world of expectations.

I'm particularly drawn to the dances of the Middle East and India. There's a vibrancy to them, a raw and passionate expression, that touches my soul and speaks to the woman in me. The woman who loves, laughs, cries and feels anger. A woman who can sometimes— just sometimes—allow herself to feel despair over the possibility of never having children of her own. Who can feel the anger and guilt that come from living under the shadow of other people's wants, and a conservative, strict upbringing. When I dance, especially when I move to the intoxicating and ancient rhythms of Middle Eastern and Indian music, I feel a new me inside. In dance I feel myself speaking not only of my own joys, aspirations and fears, but those of all women past and present. When I dance, I am no less Woman than my oldest sister or any other mother.

The years march on. The insurance business is as stifling as any "stable" job could be. I'm responsible, well liked in the office and have moved up. There's room to move higher—and a fair certainty that I will. My hard work has earned me a mortgage, a car, beautiful decorations and some exquisite antique dolls who stare at me accusingly from chairs that a child might occupy. I've had a relationship with an abusive man. I've had close brushes with marriage. But I'm still single. The biological clock is ticking faster and faster toward the dreaded

Forty. Sometimes when I sing at weddings, it's painful. I wonder if that will ever be me pledging my eternal love to another. It can be even worse at funerals, where my songs mark the passing of generations. People ask me about children as if I'm "supposed" to be a mother. Sometimes it feels like I'm being judged, as if I'm not fulfilling my natural role in womanhood. As if to be childless is some kind of criminal failure. This is oppression of the cruelest kind. Men are allowed to make babies—or not—with wild abandon, beholden only to their wages and their consciences.

My wages have built a collection of music of other cultures. I've studied Middle Eastern and Indian dance with top instructors and artists. I've even been hired as a belly dancer for numerous events, and business is picking up. It pays well, which is good because the training, travel and costumes are very expensive. *Maqams, tablas, sagats,* Orientale, Persian, Bollywood, Bhangra and Mujra have become words in this American Catholic girl's vocabulary, and I study the cultures that have produced these magical forms of expression. Through them all I feel the same mystical spirit that I imagined as a child—a link that connects the deepest feelings of all women, everywhere, through the ages.

At night, after another confining day in the office, I dance out my frustration in a special room in my home. The music envelopes me and my feelings come out in my movements. *This is who I want to be,* I think as I twirl and sway. A *woman who is free of the judgment of others, free of the internal and external pressure to be or do anything for anyone.* I finally realize that I need to make a break from the person I am.

Forty. My family and friends think I'm crazy to give notice at my secure job and start my own business as a professional belly dancer. Some of them don't get it; they think that this form of dance is sexual, degrading or "nice as a hobby, but you need a real job." But it's none of those things, and their words show a painful, unfair prejudice that widens the divide of our fragile relationships. In fact, belly dance is anything but degrading. It's a fine art, the ballet of multiple cultures—

just not the one I was born into. And I am an artist. I've put in the time and effort to train myself, and I'm going for it. I intend to step out from under the expectations, opinions and conservative dogma that have crushed my spirit for so long. I'm going to live for myself. It's *my* life. I'm going to live it on my terms.

When I walk out of the insurance office for the last time, I feel like I am being born into a new self and a new world.

Today, I'm a full time, professional artist. With every performance, I push myself out onto a stage into the unknown. But the unknown is beautiful when you're exploring it for yourself. I'm not a model employee with a secure job, and that's okay. I'm not that conservative, guilt ridden person of a few years ago, and that's okay. I'm not a wife and mother, and that's okay, too. My new direction has taken me to study and perform around the United States, and I've realized a life-long dream by performing at the John F. Kennedy Center for the Performing Arts. It can be frightening to be self employed, especially doing something as physically demanding as this, where a twisted ankle or a hip injury could put me out of business. But it's worth the risk, because I *am* my own job and, more important, I am my own person. Letting go of the need to define myself as other expect has been incredibly liberating. It's better to just be me. My antique dolls no longer haunt me, but make me happy.

Now I have to go — my cue is coming up. The music is growing, louder still, and I can feel the anticipation of the audience as they wait for me to perform. I peek through the curtain and see many women in the crowd: mothers, daughters, even a couple of grandmothers. There are no doubt some present who are dreading their own biological clocks; dreading being childless; dreading going home to families or husbands or boyfriends who make them wish they were something or someone else. I smile. Their collective energy will feed my spirit and I'll dance for all of these women, as I always do. It's okay for us to be who we are. Because, mothers or not, we are all goddesses.

The biological clock has pushed me to the cliff, and I'm not going to fall. I'm going soar.

A native of Washington, D.C., Shadiyah has performed locally and nationally in venues that include embassies, universities, weddings and corporate events. She has been featured in *The Washington Post*, *Washingtonian*, and *Washington Masala*.

The Best of All Worlds

Cara Holman

As a child, I had it all figured out. When I grew up, I would marry, have five children of my own, and balance family with a full-time career. After all, why not? That's exactly what my mom did, and she made it look easy. It was many years before I learned that mom made it look easy because she was extraordinary.

My parents were anomalies in our middle-class suburban neighborhood on Long Island. They saw the value of education first hand, as the children of immigrant parents, and raised us five kids to the highest standards of scholarship. We had to be the only family on the block where an A– was considered a bad grade. I remember once coming home from school when I was in the second or third grade, and proudly showing my dad a spelling test where I received a score of 98. "What happened to the other two points?" Dad quipped, only half joking.

Dinners at our home were always filled with lively discussion, whether the topic was the events of our daily lives, current events, or my parents' favorite, a debate about math and science. Mom was a math teacher and Dad was a medical researcher, so it was a pretty deep debate. I'd have to say it was usually a draw.

I traded the east coast for the west when I headed off for college, joining my two sisters in California to attend Stanford University. Following in Mom's footsteps, I majored in mathematics, deviating

Cara Holman

only far enough to pick up a Master's degree in computer engineering as well. My future was looking assured, especially when I embarked on a career as a systems analyst straight out of college, something my parents surely approved of. I also met Mr. Right, and at the age of twenty-four, with a career and a husband in hand, I only needed my five children to complete my childhood aspirations.

There was always an implicit, or perhaps not quite so implicit, expectation in my family that we all continue on with post-graduate work, earn a doctorate like my dad and pursue research careers. With this expectation working quietly on my subconscious, I made the decision to leave the work force to enter a Ph.D. program in computer science at the University of Washington. At this point, it seemed like I was on the fast track for a career in academia.

I was well into working on my thesis when my carefully laid plans went awry. I can't really say I heard the tick of my biological clock, but I did find myself looking longingly at other people's babies, and would often walk through the baby aisles in stores, fingering the adorable little out-fits. Unexpectedly, the baby bug had bitten me, and naïve as I was, I imagined that my life would remain relatively unchanged after becoming a mother, with me continuing with my research while my hypothetical baby played happily on its own by my side.

Well, a year later, there I was with my flesh and blood baby, an irresistible little boy who clearly had his own ideas—and playing quietly on a blanket with toys while I worked was not one of them. My parenting books assured me he was "assertive," not "demanding," but demanding or assertive, he sure did seem to have a lot of needs. Gone were my fantasies of working full time on my research while being the perfect mom.

"How did you manage five of us and a career, Mom?" I asked in desperation. "I'm struggling with one here."

Mom replied, "I left my job designing control systems for submarines to stay home and raise you in those early years. It was nearly a decade before I went back to work, and becoming a teacher enabled me to be on the same schedule as you children. And I couldn't have done it," she added, "without the support of the entire family."

So here I was at a crossroads in my life, faced with similar choices to the ones my mother had to make more than three decades earlier. Should I forge on, earning my Ph.D. straightaway, and concentrate on getting my new career established, a choice that would entail me finding child care for my son? Or should I take several years off from the work force to stay home with my son as my mother had done, and perhaps forgo the Ph.D. altogether? I agonized over the decision for months, trying to reason it all out logically. In the end, it was not logic, but gut feeling, that led me to leave school with an "Ab.D." (all but dissertation) and become a "stay-at-home" mom for my son and the subsequent children I had, which ended up totaling three. That was 23 years ago, and I've never regretted that decision.

Initially, the toughest part of my new redesigned life was that after so many years in the academic world, I was used to daily intellectual challenge, and, to put it mildly, it was an abrupt transition to suddenly find myself at home with a highly active newborn. Further, none of my closest friends had started families yet, so it was some time before I managed to acquire a new peer group and adjust to the strange new world I now inhabited. Who would ever have imagined that a baby could be so demanding? It seemed that nothing I'd learned in school seemed relevant, and I felt totally unprepared for this new endeavor.

I hadn't spent all of those years in school for nothing, however. Applying the same kind of academic discipline I had developed over the years to parenting, I soon began to read everything I could on the subject of parenting and attended parenting talks. The rest I learned "on the job." The early years of parenting didn't leave me much time to pursue outside interests, being tied to the whims of my demanding—I mean assertive—children. I found my greatest satisfaction, though, in immersing myself in motherhood and becoming an integral part of my children's lives as they grew and developed

> "Should I take several years off from the work force to stay home with my son, and perhaps forgo the Ph.D. altogether?"

in ways that seemed nothing short of miraculous. Motherhood called for skills I never realized I possessed, from psychologist to triage nurse, mediator, entertainer and social secretary, to say nothing of my emerging skills as a chauffeur.

Yes, motherhood is all-consuming, but it is also empowering, so while I did not ultimately get that Ph.D., I did find a rewarding new direction beyond being a mother. In fact, it was enrolling my children in co-op preschools that gave me the impetus to pursue the second component of my new, reinvented life: being a volunteer. Volunteerism is part and parcel of the co-op philosophy, and interestingly, I found that this model wasn't so different from the one I had grown up with. Volunteering has become my career, along with parenting, and I can't think of another career that would have given me as much satisfaction.

Cara Holman is a stay-at-home mom and community volunteer who makes her home in Portland, Oregon with her husband and the youngest of her three children. A mathematician by training, she began writing after a diagnosis of breast cancer led her to join the Women with Cancer Writing Group at Ohio State University. Her work has appeared in *Along the Journey* and in *Survivor's Review*.

PART FOUR

My Spirit Renewed

Who's In a Name

Bobbi Arduini

Age Eight

My name is Bobbi, but I answer to just about anything. My sister thinks it is fun to change my name every week or so. One week I could be Margot, and the next week Tigger. She takes care of me more than anyone else, ever since Mom went to the hospital and Dad stopped talking to us. She's a grownup, ten years older than me, ready to leave for college. Sometimes she throws big parties and I get to pump the keg. Her friends laugh and tell me that I'm going to be "cool" when I get older. I am not "cool" in elementary school. I'm "sensitive," according to my teacher. That's why I cry all the time.

Sometimes I make up my own names. I call myself Bull's Eye and pretend that I'm a brave but lost cat in search of my master. At other times I am Bandit, part of a gang of thieves known as the Cat's Claw. I always pretend I'm a boy because boys have more fun. Boys like my brothers get to go out and have fun with their friends and play little league. Girls stay home and use lots of hairspray and babysit their little sisters.

When I get tired of renaming myself, I name the trees in the yard. My favorite is Quicksilver, the tree next to the driveway that blooms fragile pink flowers every spring with petals that fall softly in big clumps onto the windshield of Mom's car. I like to climb Quicksilver's branches and pretend they are racehorses, pretend that they can take

Bobbi Arduini

me to somewhere new, somewhere I can hardly imagine but is peaceful and happy and far away from hospitals. Quicksilver takes me somewhere people don't drool or drag their feet on yellow linoleum floors, where mothers don't speak in tongues or fall backwards waiting for angels to catch them, where fathers don't go silent for months on end. Someplace where I can be very, very sensitive, but nothing makes me cry. Sometimes I sit in Quicksilver for hours, rocking the branches up and down. Nothing really changes except that some petals shake free from their flowers and drift to the ground, but I feel like I'm going somewhere. I know that I'm not, but in the slow lazy shower of soft pink raindrops, it's easy to pretend.

Age Sixteen

The cops call me a town rat. They think it's an insult, but I think it's cool. I don't like cops. They always hassle me and my friends because we look different—we wear trench coats and fishnets and dye our hair black and tattoo each other with sewing needles and pierce our eyebrows with safety pins.

My parents hassle me, too. They want me to dress "normal" and go to college. I get good grades because I like learning, but I don't really care about school. I think my parents are only concerned with how I make them look. They have no idea who I am. They don't know that I drink almost every day in the parking lot behind Caffeine Jones, or in the woods behind the bowling alley. They don't know that I'm on birth control. They don't know that I'm hell in a mosh pit. They don't know that when I'm drunk, I sometimes cut myself with the razor blades my dad leaves in the basement, and they don't know that my boyfriend Steve shoots heroin and smokes crack. They definitely don't know what Alfonsi did to me at Mark's house, how I screamed and screamed until some people broke down the door to get me out, but it was too late. I tried to tell my mom once, but she told me not tell anyone else. People might think it was my fault.

Two weeks after that, she went back into the psych ward of Good Sam. I didn't want to go visit her, but I thought my dad and sister and brothers would call me selfish, so I ended up going. She showed me watercolors she'd painted of flowers and she hugged me about a million times. I smiled and told her that I loved her, and I meant it, but when I got back home, I snuck down into the basement and went into the liquor cabinet and drank what I could of the Jack Daniels until I forgot about her and Alfonsi and Steve and the razor blades and everyone and everything else, including myself.

Sometimes I wish I really was just a town rat instead of all that I actually am.

Age Nineteen

I call myself Sparrow, because I'm small and I sing and I live on the street. I've been homeless for almost a year now. I don't really mind, though. I feel free most of the time—when I get restless, I just head to the highway, stick out my thumb, and go somewhere new. I never get too lonely, because I have my dog Laughter. He's the cutest puppy in the world, my best friend.

I can't stay in one place too long. I'm afraid that if I do, I'll start shooting dope again. When I first left home, my parents sent me to college at Tulane in New Orleans. I was only there for a month when I started using heroin. I started because my boyfriend Steve kept relapsing on it; I was tired of being so scared of something I didn't understand. Once I tried it, I completely understood why Steve kept using—it was magnificent. On heroin, I felt completely numb. I didn't care about anything. It wasn't like with drinking, where I'd black out and start crying about my mom or raging about Alfonsi.

But it didn't stay that way. My parents found out, even though they didn't want to believe it was true. They pulled me out of college and flew me back home, but they couldn't keep me: I was eighteen, an adult. I left town for New Orleans again, and even though I kinda meant to stay clean and get a job and pay for college without their help, somehow I ended up doing heroin again—and it got bad. Really bad. I found out that there are people in this world even worse than Alfonsi. A lot of people. Regularly, I started to wake up in crack houses or squats or alleyways, covered in mud and blood and bruises, and it hurt so bad inside and out that I had to get high again. Only when I got high, things always got carried away. I woke up in those places again and again and again, and always with the same hurts. So I left New Orleans. I went to Taos, where I got Laughter. When I got restless, I went to Little Rock. Then I went to Memphis. Then I went to Ann Arbor. Then I went to Boulder. Then I went to Atlanta. Then I went back to Taos.

I just keep going and going and going because I think I'm just one town ahead of my past and I'm afraid that, if I stop, the Bobbi of the past will catch up with the Sparrow of today, and I'll have to feel things that I can't feel, and I'll have to do drugs again to stop all those feelings, and bad stuff will happen while I'm on drugs that will give me worse nightmares than I already have, if that's even possible.

Besides, I like being Sparrow most of the time. Sparrow is a lot happier than Bobbi ever was. Sparrow just hitchhikes and sings and plays with her dog, and if she gets lonely sometimes, well, that's okay. The world keeps her company— the sunlight pounding down on the black asphalt, the clouds lazily taking shape overhead, the soft rustling of tree branches in the warm gentle breeze. Sparrow doesn't mind sleeping under bridges or eating out of dumpsters. Sparrow just needs to keep moving, keep moving, keep moving. She doesn't know

> "I can smell the grass like never before. It is sweet and beautiful and alive, just like me. I am Bobbi all over again, with a new life spreading out in front of me."

where she's going, but she knows that when she gets there, she won't have to worry about remembering anything ever again.

Age Twenty-Two

At the college health clinic, waiting for the results of my first HIV and Hep C test, I have no name. Instead, I have a number—4—and a lot of fear. By all rights, I *should* test positive. At twenty-two I've shared needles with countless junkies. I've slept with more men than I can even remember. I have been clean for almost eleven months—the hardest eleven months of my life—but that doesn't undo my past. It doesn't matter that I'd gotten off the streets when the malnutrition and depression caught up with me, had aced my way through college classes, making up for lost time, and am now communicating with my parents—who I *finally* realize have loved me all along—in a tender and respectful way. None of that stuff matters though, in terms of my blood, so I wait for the nurse to call me in for my results and imagine the possible lives I have in front of me.

In one life, I call all my ex-boyfriends and tell them that I have lied about getting tested before, that I have possibly killed them and I am sorry. I know "sorry" doesn't cut it and I can't deal with the guilt, so I start shooting dope again, even though it breaks my parents' hearts. I don't want to hurt them, but I don't know what else to do—I've never been good at handling things.

In that life, of course, I get a junkie boyfriend. We rob convenience stores. We shoot up in small rooms with dirty mattresses on the floor, then lie together for an eternity, silent and hardly touching. I don't get the chance to waste away because I die of an overdose in a bathroom with no electricity or running water. My boyfriend gets scared so he leaves my body there. It takes the cops a couple days to find me. They identify me by my tattoos, which is particularly painful for my dad because he never knew I had any. It makes him think about all the other things that we never knew about each other. Mom, of course, goes crazy.

In another life, I call my parents and tell them everything they never wanted to know about dirty needles and unprotected sex. At first, they are in shock; then they are furious. I bear their anger with patience and compassion, knowing I deserve nothing more. Eventually they ask me to move home. They promise to help me die with peace and dignity. It takes a while for us to adjust. But we keep trying.

My mom and I discover that we both like to garden. I tell her about naming all the trees when I was a kid and we both cry a little, because even though we lived together, we still missed so much of each other.

At night, I watch baseball games on TV with my dad. I learn all the correct lingo, memorize the stats with him. We root for the Yankees and passionately hate the Red Sox. We don't talk about our feelings directly, but we don't need to. There is enough in baseball to cover everything. And when I die, it is at home, in the twin bed I slept in until I was eighteen. My parents hover near me, loving me and regretting me. And when I die, I die beautifully and bravely and quietly, and I do it that way for them.

"Number Four?"

The nurse looks at me, her bright red lips spreading over sparkling teeth, as surreal as a toothpaste commercial. She ushers me into a back room decorated with a poster of a puppy dog sitting in a field of sunflowers, smiles, and tells me that I have nothing to worry about.

Nothing?

Absolutely nothing.

You're sure?

Positive.

The word "positive" is loaded with meaning; the inherent symbolism in the moment is almost overwhelming to me, but I don't say anything about that. Instead, I smile back mechanically and thank her. I leave the room, sign some forms as Number Four, and walk outside.

Outside in the warm early October air, I see mud from recent rain. I can smell the grass like never before. It is sweet and beautiful and precious and alive, just like me, just like me.

And just like that, I am Bobbi all over again, with a new life spreading out in front of me, and what to do with it, what to do?

Age Twenty-Seven

A student waits outside my classroom door. He is a bit awkward in the way that many sixteen year old boys are–gangly, shaggy- haired, serious face dotted with a little acne. It is the first day of school, and he looks more prepared than I feel. He, at least, knows what to bring–paper and pencil and backpack and schedule. I brought my three page typed single-spaced lesson plan that I thought would last the entire hour of class but would soon discover takes up only thirty minutes.

"English III?" I ask him. He gives me a curt nod, taking in my suit and probably my relative youth, as compared to other teachers.

"What's your name?" I ask him, unlocking the door.

"Steven," he says quietly.

I reach out my hand. "My name is Bobbi," I reply, completely forgetting that I am now a *teacher* and do not give out my first name. "I'm mean, Bobbi Arduini. *Ms.* Arduini."

Steven looks confused, but he doesn't say anything, just obediently follows me into the classroom and takes a seat as far away from me as possible. When he is transferred out of my class the next week, I am incredibly relieved that I won't have to be reminded of that first awkward interaction. For now, though, I write "MS. ARDUINI" on the overhead projector in bright blue ink, wondering if I will ever feel like I am that adult-sounding, respectable, employable name.

If I could see ahead in time, I would know that I had nothing to worry about—that, ironically, teaching would come as naturally to me as drug use once did. In a few years time I will see the inherent potential of each student's unique face, knowing that within every one is an entire universe of possibilities, tragic and comic and magnificent. And I will write them recommendations and read their poems and correct their grammar, and we will tell each other stories, and I will do my best to exceed their expectations. They will know that I am much more than Ms. Arduini, and I'll know that they are *so much more* than names on my roster, and sometimes when they are talking to me, I'll just look at them and think—it was worth it. It was worth it, after all. I will watch as my beautiful students write in their journals, and I will wonder how it was possible to be so many people in only one life.

Bobbi Arduini lives in Oakland, California. She received a Master of Fine Arts in Creative Nonfiction from Saint Mary's College and now teaches high school English.

The Road to Tena

Mary Fifield

The bus lurched down the unpaved road from the Ecuadorian Andes into the rainforest, and I saw a sign as we rounded a curve. It was a crudely-made sign in the form of an arrow. It said, simply, TENA. And I felt something certain within me—I knew this was home. Why I knew that I couldn't say, since I'd grown up in Nevada and California, places that couldn't have been more different from the Amazon. But there was no questioning that feeling.

Tena is a small provincial capital on the edge of the rainforest, typical of a lot of underdeveloped towns in Latin America: rebar jutting from unfinished second stories; gaping holes in the sidewalks (where there are sidewalks); undrinkable water; reckless drivers; indigenous women selling jungle fruit on the corners to make a little extra money to feed their kids; rich people sequestered in their comparatively posh neighborhoods.

Tena is also surrounded by the infinite green of the Amazon jungle, where the Kichwa and other indigenous groups have lived for generations. That is where I spend much of my time working in community development. On a typical day, I might slog through ankle-high mud to talk to women in a thatched-roof hut; be served a bowl of soup made from "jungle meat" (usually a large rodent though sometimes monkey or toucan); build a composting toilet out of cement and chicken wire; teach a group of community leaders how to fill out a project plan; and

Mary Fifield

make a fool of myself trying to speak Kichwa. Then I'll return home, pour myself a beer, and sit out on the patio watching the sunset, listening to salsa music and my neighbors' barking dogs.

In the serenity of those evenings, I sometimes find myself reflecting on the life I lived for 35 years and the one I'm leading now. Making your way in a different culture, speaking two different languages, and living in a rural area all present challenges, but I don't have any regrets and I don't take my experience here for granted. I learn something new every day, whether it's the reason for peeling an orange before you suck the juice out of it (local oranges have a bitter oil on the peel that will make your lips numb) or the most effective way to complain about poor customer service at the phone company. Sometimes I just learn new Kichwa or Spanish vocabulary or another chapter in Ecuador's complex political history. I constantly gain new respect for the natural environment, for the challenge of striking a balance between human needs and those of the rainforest, an ecosystem that is both overpowering and threatened. Every day I am reminded what it means to live in the moment.

My mother died from a brain aneurism when I was thirty. It was a traumatic shock from which our family has still not recovered completely almost nine years later. But that alone was not the trigger that caused me to reevaluate my life. While working in one gray cubicle after another in Seattle, I'd been fighting a losing battle to forge my career as a writer, succumbing to a desperation that I was giving up on myself. I was single and longing for real love and meaningful companionship. I wanted to travel but was afraid I didn't have the guts to do it. I was unsure about my future and doubting my own capacity to shape it.

A few months after my mother's death, my brother, sister, and I went to see relatives in western Pennsylvania for Christmas. During those holiday family visits, going from living rooms to family rooms to restaurants, I saw myself against a backdrop of my cousins, all younger than I and married with kids, stable jobs, mortgages, t-ball league games and barbecues on the lake. Most of them had never been to the West Coast, let alone out of the country. I imagined they looked at me with a mixture of confusion and pity, and I could understand it—they were happy, and I was not.

That was the point when I realized one of the things my mother's death was meant to teach me. My need for security had pushed me down the familiar road of the American middle class, where I had convinced myself that I could find a way to live comfortably and still achieve dreams that were fundamentally incompatible with the quest for a full-time job, a mortgage, and good schools for one's kids. In reality, I was failing at middle class life: I didn't want to be chained to a desk for fifty hours a week or have responsibilities that would obligate me to stay there. Yet I was too afraid to stake everything and go out on my own, so I was failing at achieving the dream most important to me.

When I returned to work a few days later, I could see very clearly where my life was headed. I was so agitated and beside myself that I had to go home sick. I made plans that day to start over from scratch. Changing my life had become a matter of emotional survival.

I started with what, at the time, was my biggest fear: traveling by myself in Central America. A few years earlier I'd traveled to Costa Rica for three weeks. Now I wanted to visit other countries, study more Spanish, and let myself explore.

> "Maybe I was a mediocre person who would live a mediocre life... I had to grow up and face the reality that I could very well fail at what was most important to me."

Guatemala had the cheapest language schools, but I also believed it was the most dangerous country I planned to visit. I wasn't an experienced backpacker and my Spanish was basic at best, so I debated for weeks on whether I should begin my journey there. In the end, my frugality barely trumped my fear. Landing in Guatemala City, which I'd read was a hotbed of robberies and homicides, I was a nervous wreck. But once I found my bus to Antigua and ascended the windy road into the highlands, I knew I'd made the best decision yet of my life.

I spent five weeks in Guatemala studying Spanish at a school that opened originally to teach Spanish to Americans who came as human rights volunteers during the Guatemalan civil war. I learned a lot about that bloody conflict. I met interesting people, saw the spectacular countryside, and traveled to the Ixil Triangle, where massacres had occurred. There I saw a painting on a church wall of indigenous men crucified on crosses and a few words of homage to the injustice and tragedy of their deaths. Though Ixil in particular carried a foreboding air, I was grateful to have visited it.

After more than a month in Guatemala, having firmly established my solo traveler's legs, I journeyed to Honduras, Belize and Mexico, where I discovered I had a knack as well as a passion for finding and exploring new places. Three months after I began, I flew back to Seattle, where most of my belongings were in storage. Before my trip, I'd planned to reestablish myself there, but soon I realized that changing my life would require more than simply taking a long vacation and getting a new job and new apartment in Seattle. I'd also fallen in love with a man I met in Guatemala who lived in the San Francisco Bay Area, where I had friends and family as well. Instead of moving my things from storage to a new apartment, I packed them in a U-Haul and headed back to California, where I'd spent half my life.

But my life in Oakland fell apart before it started to come together. My new boyfriend and I broke up; it took almost a year before I had clients for my new consulting business in marketing communications; many of my friends had gotten married and were busy with their own lives, and I was living alone and working out of my apartment. Some days I had to walk to the corner coffeehouse and order a latte just to hear my own voice. Living off savings was stressful, but even scarier was the possibility that I wasn't destined for greatness, after all. Maybe I was a mediocre person who would live a mediocre life made even more pathetic by her own delusions of grandeur. During the first year or so in Oakland, I had to grow up and face the reality that I could very well fail at what was most important to me.

The blessing about not having paying work was that I had hours every week to pursue other interests. I wrote, went to readings, researched Guatemalan history, and began to explore my spiritual needs. That last turned out to be another lesson from my mother's death. She was a seeker of the most surprising kind. From her polyester pants, Kmart tennis shoes, and circa-1965 bouffant hairdo that she never saw fit to update, you would never have guessed that she meditated daily for an hour, practiced astral projection, kept altars of crystals and shells, and read every New Age text she could get her hands on. I recognized that we believed in some of the same fundamental principles, especially that love is the energy that guides the universe and that our job is to let that energy manifest through us. So while I wasn't drawn to the same people or books, I began to keep the promise I made to my mother as she lay unconscious in her hospital bed: that I'd continue her spiritual legacy as long as I could do it in my own way.

After a couple of years, I hit my stride in Oakland. I had enough consulting clients to pay my bills. I had a life full of hobbies such as playing drums, reading, cooking, hiking, spending time with my friends and traveling. Then, in October of 2004, one of my clients, an international health non-profit organization, sent me to the Ecuadorian Amazon to write about their project there. Though I'd always wanted to travel to Ecuador and Peru, I was inexplicably nervous on the plane. An American friend of mine had recently died in a car accident in Quito, and though I didn't believe I'd meet the same fate, on some level I must have been aware of my own mortality and maybe the phase of mid-life I was entering. To calm myself, I wrote in my journal and decided I just had to open my heart up to love in its many forms.

Love came to me in a village about a 30-minute canoe ride from Tena. He was a Kichwa man who worked for another development organization, and we discovered almost immediately that despite our completely different backgrounds we had an easy compatibility and a lot of things in common. In the early days I wondered if we were just attracted to the exoticism in each other, but we ended up having a complex, intense relationship that ultimately helped me become more truly myself and enjoy the effort of maintaining an open heart.

After that first trip, I returned to Ecuador a few times on my own. About a year later, the founder of the health organization asked me to step in as executive director. I considered it reluctantly—I didn't want the responsibility or the restriction on my time. But I was also growing tired of marketing, and I wanted to have the opportunity to spend more time in Ecuador. I wanted to see what the country meant to me apart from my love relationship, which was coming to an end.

Ultimately I accepted the new job and spent the following year traveling constantly. Even for someone with gypsy blood, the schedule was exhausting. I didn't have a home base in either country, and I now needed that. Walking down a residential street in my Oakland neighborhood one evening, I realized that the fantasy I'd begun to form about my domestic life butted heads with the very same challenges I faced in Seattle. In my current line of work I could not afford a mortgage on a modest house in an urban neighborhood where I would want to live. So if I wanted to free myself from rent increases, I'd have to change my career, which I didn't want to do, or live in a suburban neighborhood where I'd be dependent on my car and isolated from the variety of urban life. That variety was the only thing that kept me from feeling overwhelmed by the consumerism and increasing homogeneity of American culture, which I observed more sharply since traveling in South America.

Once I made the decision to move to Ecuador, it took another year or so to discover how I could make it happen. The universe must have been conspiring, though, because a solution arose that satisfied everyone. The organization decided to create new on-the-ground positions in order to expand its operations, so I took the position in Ecuador. I was excited not only to begin my new life, but to continue developing a program I had started as executive director to support projects designed and managed by communities, for communities.

Communities responded enthusiastically to the idea of taking more control over their own destiny, and I started to see how the same approach could be used to help Kichwa people, who have been discriminated against for centuries, reclaim their traditional role as environmental stewards and in the process reclaim some of their pride. But the idea fell outside the scope of the health non-profit, so some colleagues of mine and I made the decision to start our own, Amazon Partnerships Foundation. Through small grants and intensive project management training, we work with Kichwa communities that want to protect this irreplaceable rainforest and revive their conservation-based culture.

Along with everything else here, the work teaches me daily lessons about myself and my life. I don't find myself gazing out the window wondering what I am really meant to do and whether I have the courage to do it. That's not to say that this path is without its pits of quicksand. The specter of new, large-scale oil and mining projects is a constant threat, and those in power are slow to understand the long-term value of a healthy rainforest in averting the worst effects of climate change, not to mention the ever-narrowing window of opportunity to do something about it. This worry can sometimes be distracting, just as the noise of consumer culture did in the U.S. But letting go of my delusions of grandeur has helped me. I will always be just one person, and I will do what one person can do. Having learned the lessons of my mother's death, I take risks and seek the path of love, letting the jungle remind me that life happens only in each moment, regardless of human frenzy.

The experience of living here is more complex than I could have imagined riding down that spine-jarring road from the Andes. But like the sign that pointed me in this direction, it is real and meaningful. Considering that meaning is what I seek out of life, I suppose it's not so surprising that I ended up here. Love's compass has its own logic.

Mary Fifield's writing has appeared in *Colere, Intercom,* and *Midway Journal.* She has a Master of Fine Arts in creative writing from San Diego State University. She is Executive Director of Amazon Partnerships Foundation and lives in the Ecuadorian Amazon. She writes about indigenous culture, environmental issues, and her adventures as an expatriate in the Amazon.

Five Year Plan

Beth Morrissey

"And just one last question," the interviewer said with a kind smile. It was the first time she'd spoken throughout the whole thing, and I had already mentally written off any chance of her asking anything at all. She'd actually yawned when I'd entered the room, and I had her pegged as the woman included on the panel simply to make up numbers. I took a deep breath. I knew what was coming. There wasn't an interviewer around who didn't save the dreaded "five year plan" question until the end, and for whatever reason it was always the bored ones who asked it.

"Alright," I said flatly, trying to stay upbeat while my fingers involuntarily clutched my armrest until the knuckles turned a dull white. I glanced at them and had to remind myself to loosen my grip. I folded my hands in my lap and waited.

"Now, Elizabeth, where do you see yourself in five years? What would you like to be doing?"

There it was, a question so big and unwieldy it was the proverbial elephant in the room. Crazily, the first thought that entered my head was that the woman had a gruesome smear of red lipstick on one of her canine teeth which made her look particularly menacing. I shivered and her smile grew wider. Sadist.

I took a minute to compose myself, agonizing the whole time. Why hadn't I prepared better? Why hadn't I come up with some stock answer about being a valuable member of the team, sharing my knowledge with others, anything other than the blank slate that was currently lodged in my head? Grasping at straws, I thought back over what I was doing five years ago. School librarian. I thought back five years before that. Social care worker. Another five years before, lifeguard. Panicked, I realized that there was no common thread, nothing to indicate that I had a career path or even a career progression. Hell, nothing to indicate that I actually had a career instead of just a series of jobs.

> "I don't know where I'd like to be in five years, but I know who I hope to be. I hope to still be the kind of woman who follows her heart. I hope to be happy."

While the panel looked on expectantly, I felt a strange calm descend. No, that wasn't right. Of course there was a common thread. Each and every job made me happy. Each and every job paid my bills. Each and every job let me interact with others, teach them something and help them grow. More than that, each job let others teach me and help me grow. So it might not be the tidiest of career tracks, but whose was? Who really knew what they'd want or need in five years time? Who could plan for the lightning bolt that brought their true love or the rolling thunder that revealed a chronic disease? Who could foresee the book they'd read that would change their lives or the child's smile that would touch their hearts?

I looked into the closed faces of the panel and knew that they'd never understand. They were here for one thing and one thing only, to choose the next drone that would fit perfectly as a cog in their machine. They didn't want someone who could see possibilities, they wanted someone who prepared for probabilities. They didn't want me.

I plastered a smile on my face and spoke honestly from the bottom of my heart.

"I don't know where I'd like to be in five years, but I know *who* I hope to be. I hope to still be the kind of woman who follows her heart instead of her head. I hope to be happy."

I watched the panel glance at each other, confused. I smiled wider. I didn't know what I actually meant, either, but I knew that it wouldn't matter if I reinvented myself one time or twenty times in the next five years. As long as I was doing it with all my heart, I'd be just fine.

Beth Morrissey is a freelance writer, researcher and tutor in Dublin, Ireland. She's lived, studied and worked on three continents and is eagerly anticipating her next reinvention — whatever it may be.

The Scars We Carry

Marcia Trahan

"We'll make the incision right about here," the surgeon said, drawing his index finger lightly across the base of my throat. "Now, I know you don't like that idea."

Actually, the idea of having a four-inch-long scar on my neck wasn't my biggest concern at that moment. I was more unnerved by the notion of having my throat sliced open. A biopsy had found abnormal cells in a nodule on my thyroid gland. Ninety percent of these nodules were benign, I'd been told, but the only way to be certain was to remove them, which in my case involved removing the entire right lobe of the thyroid. The prospect of surgery scared me more than the possibility that I had cancer. I was thirty-five; I'd always been healthy. Of course I would fall into that 90-percent-benign category.

"You're young," the surgeon continued, "so you don't have wrinkles — yet." He grinned, and I forced a little laugh. "We make the cut where there's already a line in your skin, so that as you age, the skin sort of sags over the scar. Then it's less noticeable."

"Well," I said, "I guess that'll be something to look forward to."

No matter how he tried to downplay the scar, it was no small thing to me. It would be something to hide. Hiding: I knew how to do that only too well. I kept shame and fear and insecurity locked away beneath a polished surface. Very few people knew of my rocky childhood, my low

Marcia Trahan

self regard, my struggles with near-crippling anxiety, the poorly handled credit card and student loan debt that now kept me nailed to a
desk in a cubicle, plugging data into Excel spreadsheets instead of pursuing the writer's life full-bore. I slipped into my business casual best
every morning like a false skin, feeling a mixture of revulsion and
relief. I'd become adept at keeping deep dark secrets early, when I first
learned that earning straight A's could fool adults into thinking everything was fine. After two decades of practice, I'd perfected the role of
the invulnerable achiever. The average observer saw a bright, capable,
confident woman who'd long ago laid any demons to rest. I rarely permitted glimpses of the real me, the one who could never be smart
enough, accomplished enough, strong enough.

How would I deal with this? I simply could not be viewed as vulnerable, could not allow my skin to suggest the injuries I'd sustained on the inside. In the days between my surgical consultation and the actual operation, I found myself thinking about what the scar would look like. But I took some comfort in what the surgeon had told me. A thin pink line? How hard could that possibly be to hide?

The surgery was a breeze; I went home the next day, surprised at how little pain I felt. Three days later, I stood in front of my bathroom mirror and removed the dressing. Another surprise: the scar, the one I'd told myself I didn't care about, was bigger, redder, and more raised than I'd imagined. My heart dropped at the first sight of that Frankenstein-ish pucker of cut flesh. It underscored my chin, like the mark of a middle school English teacher's angry red pen.

I showed Andy, my partner. "It looks *awful*," I moaned.

"Oh, honey, no, it doesn't. It's incredible, really. It hardly looks like anything happened."

I smiled ruefully. This was the man who, a few years earlier, hadn't noticed that I'd gained twenty-five pounds. "Did you?" he'd said when I pointed it out. "I'd never have known. I guess it's because you're tall." *Love may be blind*, I thought, *but the rest of the world isn't. How on earth am I going to be able to hide this?*

The weekend after the surgery, before I returned to my job as an office assistant, I bought a silk scarf. A muted shade of plum, it nicely complemented my fall wardrobe of reds, pinks, and purples. Donning the scarf was like performing a magic trick. I wound it several times around my neck and *voila!* The scar disappeared, and my previous self, Healthy Young Woman, returned.

"What a pretty scarf," the women at work commented. I'd told two people in the office that I was having surgery, but I didn't say what for.

Exactly one week after the procedure, I returned to the hospital for what I expected would be a quick follow-up visit with the surgeon.

When he entered the exam room, I saw that his usual impish grin was gone, and I knew. *Papillary carcinoma.* A new term to add to my expanding medical vocabulary. This type of thyroid cancer was 98 to 99 percent treatable, the surgeon said. He would need to reopen my still-healing incision and remove the remaining left half of my thyroid; it might also contain cancer cells, too small for tests to detect.

> "Maybe this self-inflicted inflammation was the message I'd always needed to absorb, all of my life: Stop hiding."

Dazed, I left the office and collapsed into Andy's arms, weeping. A storm of emotions hit me: shock over the diagnosis, relief that it wasn't something worse, grief for the always-healthy self who now seemed gone for good. What I told no one, not even Andy, was that I also grieved for the permanently lost, unmarred surface of youth. The scar, I assumed, would surely be enlarged by another visit to the operating room. It would announce my loss to every stranger on the street.

The second surgery went as smoothly as the first one had. Three tiny carcinomas were found in the left lobe of my thyroid, but there was no evidence that the cancer had spread to other areas. Remarkably, the scar stayed the same size. Still, doctors, nurses, my sisters and Andy were the only people I allowed to see it. "Wow, it looks *great*. The surgeon did an amazing job," everyone kept saying, as if I were some miraculous case of reconstructive surgery. They were right; the surgeon *had* done an amazing job. Two surgeries, one slender, neat scar? Big flipping deal. I'd been dealt one of the most treatable forms of cancer. This was no brush with mortality, not really. I ought to be grateful, I told myself sternly. I had no right to complain.

Even as I reminded myself how lucky I was, I bought two more scarves: shiny, patterned in pinks and grays. I couldn't hide the fact of my cancer from myself, but I could hide it from nearly everyone else.

Was I right to do this? I thought of all the brave women who bared their mastectomy scars for the camera. Shouldn't I be brave enough to reveal my comparatively puny scar? Or did I have a *responsibility* to keep it hidden? If I left the scar uncovered, would it seem as if I were asking for sympathy I didn't really deserve? I couldn't begin to answer these questions. Until I could, I opted for covering up.

Eventually, the quandary solved itself. As a frigid Vermont winter slowly edged into spring, I felt constrained and overheated with my neck all wrapped up. I found myself constantly reaching up to check that the scar was safely concealed; often, it wasn't. No matter how artfully I tucked and tied and readjusted the slippery fabric, it kept riding up, leaving the scar partially uncovered.

It dawned on me that I wouldn't be able to wear a scarf at all when summer came. The skin around the scar still felt tender and tingly; I didn't dare use any of the over-the-counter products that promised to "minimize" the bright colors of injury. In a last-ditch effort, I dabbed on the same concealer I used for the circles under my eyes. I'd always appreciated the honesty of that term, "concealer": a frank acknowledgement of a woman's need to hide what she thinks are flaws. It was the only makeup I still used on a daily basis. Concealer didn't completely cover my scar, but it muted that shrieking shade of pink. You could tell that something was there, but only if you looked closely— and not even paranoid me thought that anyone would stop to study the ridged terrain of my skin.

Hah! I'd performed another magic trick. I could have it both ways: I was no longer denying that the scar existed, but I wasn't letting it call attention to itself, either. I went to work scarf-less for the first time, my scar hidden in plain sight.

The next morning, I faced the mirror, concealer wand at the ready, and felt my stomach muscles clench. The makeup had irritated the skin around the scar. What had been a thin line was now a broad swath of pink.

I put down the bottle of concealer and looked again at my reflection: my naked face, my bared neck. Were they really so bad the way they were? So I had purple patches under my eyes; I'd had them since childhood, and they'd darkened during my thirties. So I had a scar. So what? Had I really believed I'd make it to forty without visible evidence of life's bumps and bruises? Well, yeah, I had.

Maybe this self-inflicted inflammation was the message I'd always needed to absorb, all of my life: *Stop hiding*. Maybe I should stop pondering rights and responsibilities, stop thinking of my scar as some sort of public statement. Maybe I could begin to learn not to care about what other people might or might not think of my so-called flaws.

I went to work, leaving my scar plainly visible. I won't claim I wasn't nervous as hell, that I didn't start to panic when I thought someone might be staring at my neck, that I mostly kept my head bowed as I whisked down the halls. But I can truthfully say that the bravado I'd playacted for years started to grow for real that day. The old saw about necessity being the mother of invention neglects to mention that necessity also breeds courage.

It's been more three years since I stopped the cover-up act, and no one has ever asked me about the scar, which has faded to a softer shade of pink. Andy insists it's "hardly noticeable." My guess is that many people notice it, but feel it would be inappropriate to comment. It's still possible that someone, at some point, will ask, and I'm not sure how I'll feel or what I'll say.

Admittedly, I'm not wishing for wrinkles to appear anytime soon, but when they do arrive, I'll be better prepared for them—and not because they'll make my scar less obvious. No anti-wrinkle creams for me, thanks. Revealing the scar has meant the beginning of self-acceptance. Yeah, I'm closing in on forty. I'm sad about what I've lost, and nervous and excited about the future. Yes, I've had cancer. I still have days when I'm swept away by anxiety and self-criticism, but I'm proudly aware of the fact that I'm a survivor, stronger than I ever gave myself credit for. What would I gain by trying to hide these truths? Why would I want to pretend I'm someone else? It's a relief to reveal the real me at last, to open my true self to others.

In allowing others to see the evidence of my injury, I'm learning to embrace myself as I am, my life for the fragile gift that it is. It helps to remember that each of us has been injured in some way. The scars we carry are proof that we've lived, that we can be wounded and still survive.

Marcia Trahan is a freelance editor and a graduate of the Bennington Writing Seminars' Master of Fine Arts program. Her work has appeared in literary journals including *Fourth Genre*, *Full Circle*, *Anderbo*, and *Clare*. She is currently working on a collection of personal essays, *The Most Livable City*.

House of Excess

Kieren Van Den Blink

A few years ago, after graduating from college, I found myself needing some extra income. I'd moved from New York City to Los Angeles and was craving steady work. So when a friend referred me to a Westside family for a tutoring job, I jumped at the chance.

At the time, I was adrift. I had just finished a successful Broadway debut, understudying three roles in *The Diary of Anne Frank*, starring Natalie Portman and directed by James Lapine. We ran for almost nine months. It was my very first acting gig. I was prosperous, I had my own apartment in the West Village, I was a signed client of the William Morris Agency, I'd performed before thousands of people, and I was a recent Ivy League graduate. Los Angeles beckoned and away I went.

But in spite of it all, I was terribly sad. My mom had died a few years before, and I was having a very hard time getting past it. My sadness was so deep that at times it consumed me. I'd wear sunglasses so people couldn't see my eyes. I missed my mother terribly and felt her absence as strongly as I'd once felt her loving presence. The hole left by her passing had become a void that sucked the joy out of everything in my life. Guilt was also leeching my spirit as I achieved things that she would never be able to celebrate with me. As my sadness deepened, I knew I needed a break from acting. I needed a job. I needed to breathe and not be so ambitious for once. This job tutoring a sixteen year-old girl in Brentwood seemed like the perfect medicine.

Kieren Van Den Blink

When I arrived at the family's tree-lined street, I was buzzed into a yard with a deep blue pool. A woman with dark, attractive features and the body of a teenager brought me in to greet her two daughters. They both had dark brown hair—tousled in a carefully coiffed kind of way—and they were friendly, excited even, to have someone around who was older than they were but younger than their parents. I entered their kitchen, three dogs lapping at my feet, prepared to tackle essays with the sophomore or maybe math with the seventh grader.

The 16-year-old and I went upstairs to her dimly lit room. It was littered with used-up candles, empty water bottles, bags of Terra chips and vegan cookies. We began with an essay she was writing for English class. We got to know one another in between bites of snacks. Her mother even brought up a tray with her daughter's dinner—exactly what she's asked for: cooked beets, steamed carrots, and marinated tofu. We sipped on bottles of flat water. After we were done, she said she felt fat.

That same evening, I was invited to move in. Free food and housing, their mother promised, if the kids could come to my room for tutoring whenever necessary. I pictured the girls knocking on my bedroom door like Jehovah's Witnesses, stacks of books in their hands, ruthless attempts at conversation. A warning light flickered in my mind. And I politely declined.

But I did become a regular visitor. When their parents were out, the girls and I would open the doors of the kitchen pantry and simply stand before it. In these moments, we drooled like Pavlov's dogs over our favorite teas, chips, chocolate candy and cookies. And then we'd journey to the fridge where we'd eat the kiwi, sliced apples, bright red cherries and tofu cheese slices.

With her little sister left to study on her own and her parents oblivious, the older girl and I would climb the stairs to her bedroom, where I'd listen while she cried like a child. She'd lean on my shoulder, tears spilling onto the strap of my tank top, her body slumped on the bed like a disjointed stuffed animal. Most nights she said she didn't feel well—her parents were infuriating her, or it was the anniversary of her grandmother's death or she had a stomachache. I had her write about her pain. It was palpable; it hung over her bed like a mosquito net, capturing her fears, making her itch.

I'd sworn secrecy to this weary-eyed teenager, but I grew concerned as her sadness became a normal part of our tutoring sessions. One night I pulled her mother aside as I was leaving.

"Your daughter seems very unhappy."

Her mother asked why, as if I were a nuisance.

"I don't know."

"The most important thing," the mother continued, "is that she do well her junior year."

My tutoring hours were increasing, often exceeding four hours a day. I enjoyed the good money and good food, but I had gone from tutor to therapist in a matter of weeks. I probably should've charged more for my services considering I ended up calling *my* therapist on the teenager's behalf one Tuesday just before midnight after she begged me to let her throw up.

I felt for her, but as much as I didn't want to admit it, I resented her. I grew up in a New Jersey town where a tattoo shop expanded and displaced our only bakery, and my sister and I were able to attend the prestigious prep school only because we qualified for financial aid. My parents were both teachers and we always felt the money pinch. It hung in the air of our home. It pulled at our hair, tugged at our backs. She lived in a sprawling house, her closets bursting with couture and pricey hipster clothing, her own brand-new SUV in the driveway. And she could yell at her mother with abandon. In short, she had everything I didn't have as a child.

Another part of me felt deeply for her. She also lacked what I did have: the structure of a happy home life to form a solid foundation under her feet. Her parents cared, but she lived in directionless chaos. Where was her family dinner? Her homework being red-pen checked by a doting mom? Where were her family vacations? She seemed to live like an injured animal, desperate for safety. Seeing this hole in her life made me miss my mother and my childhood home all the more.

During finals week a few months later, her parents asked me to stay with her while they attended a cousin's wedding in Carmel. In the same breath, they explained how vital good scores on these exams would be to their daughter's college applications. The night before they left, her mother pulled me aside to pay me in the kitchen.

"We think she may have a borderline eating disorder."

I merely agreed. I felt as if her daughter's secret hung over me like a dark cloak; I was stifled, uneasy. Once her parents were gone, the older girl confided that she'd bought liquor and cigarettes. She'd rented some videos. One of her girlfriends was coming over to hang out by the pool. How cozy this would all be, except I was there. I have no idea if it ever occurred to her that I might possibly tell her parents, which I never did. I think she was too caught up in the moment, in being a rebel, and I unfortunately could not join the cause. I'd unwillingly become the tutor/therapist/babysitter/friend. I spent the entire evening countering her attempts to ruin her finals.

As I lay in bed that night, I felt broken literally and figuratively. I was sore-backed from running circles around this girl, and the desperate futility of her life tore at my spirit. I realized I'd never once seen the family sit down to dinner together. The parents didn't demand regular chores or dole out allowances. The family didn't enjoy any of the familiar rhythms I knew so well as a child. There was a lot of love in that house, but no one seemed to know where to put it. What she desperately needed was something I couldn't give her—discipline, routine, a delicate touch to her cancerous sadness. These midnight thoughts tore at me. I missed my loving, nurturing home. I missed my mother. I missed things that this girl had never even experienced.

> "I realized that the foundation had not crumbled with my mother's death."

But I *had* experienced them. I'd never feel my mother's warm embrace again, her words of acceptance and comfort. But I *had*. My feet would never again feel the foundation of the stable, secure home I grew up in. But now I realized that the foundation had not crumbled with my mother's death. If anything, it had given me the inner strength to walk on my own path. Lying in this bed, in this troubled home, I realized that at the other side of my loss and sadness was gratitude. Gratitude for blessings that could live on in me and continue to positively impact my life. I felt a tremendous burden lift from my spirit.

When morning came, my mind was fuzzy from lack of sleep. But I felt strangely invigorated. As I had lain there half asleep, my mind swirling with agitation over this house and its inhabitants, I'd released the crushing sadness and guilt that had so dominated my spirit. I felt free. Not free of my mother, but of the impossible dream of holding on to something and someone that were no more.

My own focus became clearer. My goals began to gel. I thought to myself, Take this young tutor, who you are in this moment, and mold her into a young woman with dreams of her own, who will do great things. You've learned when to say no, when to go, when to check in with yourself, how to walk away with your head held high, and now, to be grateful for what you have. Grateful for love that knows no eating disorders, no couture, no separate eating quarters, no yelling for discipline. Grateful for my own family, that knew no great wealth but knew the empowering joy of true togetherness. Tired as I was, as much as I cared about those girls, I was nonetheless happy that morning as I drove away from that house for the last time. Looking in the rear view mirror, I said, "I am stronger for this." I had my past and I was driving towards my future—and my mom was right there with me, where she belonged.

Kieren Van Den Blink lives in Los Angeles, California with her dog, Gatsby. A graduate of Barnard College, Columbia University, Kieren is the voice of Rogue on the popular cartoon, "Wolverine & The X-Men." She debuted on Broadway in *The Diary of Anne Frank* and will star in her first feature film in the fall of 2010. Her children's book, *Sniff* will be published in 2010 and she is completing her memoir, for which she received a Ford Foundation Grant.

Becoming a Swan

Suzan L. Wiener

Why did everyone, especially my mother and sisters, feel the need to tell me I was overweight? I cried many nights, alone in my room as their hurtful words rang in my ears. Didn't they know that I could see my girth just as well as they could? Didn't they know how awful it made me feel, how many times I'd tried to lose weight? Because of the combination of my weight and their cruel words, my self-esteem was tied into a hopeless knot with my body image, and I had become shy, withdrawn and miserable.

I had always been thin, up until the time I gave up smoking. Then I substituted chocolate for cigarettes and my weight increased accordingly. I kept looking at the thin models on television and wished I could be them. How did they do it, I wondered? I bought every diet book and went on about a hundred diets, but none of them worked because I was trapped in a vicious circle of failure and self loathing. Every day I struggled not to eat that eclair or chocolate bar, but each time I succumbed and hated myself even more. My image of myself haunted me. I even had nightmares about it, and my stomach ached because of the stress.

I didn't know what to do. I *knew* I needed to lose the weight, and not just for my looks, but for my health. My back was hurting a lot, and the pain probably would have lessened if I lost the extra pounds. I cried almost all the time. I tried finding support from my friends, but they were thin like my mother and sisters and didn't understand.

The issue came to a head with my mom's eighty-fifth birthday. I wished that I could have been excited about her party, which we planned a year in advance, but I wasn't; in fact, I was actually afraid of the upcoming event because I knew my family would take the opportunity to humiliate me. Months before the party, Mom suggested I go on a diet because she didn't want me to be embarrassed. It was more likely that *she* didn't want to be embarrassed, and I wished I had the nerve to tell her so. But I kept silent, as I always did.

> "Why would I want to do anything for them after the way they made me feel? Yes, I wanted and needed to lose the weight, but strictly for myself, not for anyone else."

Then, one night as I lay in bed agonizing about it, my feelings went beyond the hurt. The anger that had been turned inwards for so long turned the other way. I got angry at the people who were inflicting their cruelty on me. And I thought, why would I want to lose the weight for them? Why would I want to do *anything* for them after the way they made me feel for so long? Yes, I wanted and needed to lose the weight, but strictly for myself, not for anyone else.

So, armed with this new point of view, I worked at it for myself and not for my mother, or my sisters. Not for anyone but me. It was discouraging at first as diet after diet seemed to fail. Regardless of the struggle, knowing that the effort was for myself alone was enough to keep me trying. Little by little, the self-punishing feelings went away, and though I couldn't give up chocolate completely, I did manage to keep it under control. I was finally able to accept the person I was.

I managed to lose a few pounds, and I felt better about myself because I knew I was eating healthier. Maybe my family wouldn't see it or be proud of me, but I certainly was proud. I knew I looked a lot better.

When I looked in the mirror, I saw a smiling stranger instead of the frowning person who used to be me.

By the time of the party, I'd lost ten pounds. I needed to lose forty more, but it was a start, and my clothing fit well for a change. When my mother Mom saw me that night, she hugged me and exclaimed, "Susie, you look wonderful!" I hugged her back and whispered, "Thank you." I was stunned at how nice she was, and grateful that she didn't criticize me. I had a great time, and even my sisters told me I looked pretty. In fact, a few noticed my weight loss, and I was thrilled with their kind comments. But I really didn't need them to feel good about myself. Not anymore.

I learned from my experience that it doesn't matter what anyone else thinks about you; you have to like who you are in spite of any so-called faults. I'm now a complete person who can do anything I set my mind to. Because I made this effort and this change—and this success—for myself.

Suzan L. Wiener's writing has appeared in *Mature Years*, *Mature Living*, *Reader's Digest*, *FellowScript*, *Verses*, *Cross & Quill*, *Mocha Memoirs*, among others. She also writes for greeting card companies.

I Never Wanted to Be a Valkyrie

Katherina Audley

I never wanted to be a Valkyrie. Growing up as a girl in America, we're encouraged to be cute and little, like Tinkerbell. I never had a chance. I was a humongous baby. My first sentence was, "Kathy Eat Now."

Camp counselors positioned me at the base of human pyramids. Gym teachers talked me out of my Nadia Com neci dreams. When puberty hit, my ribs expanded to a horrifying 40-inch circumference while my breasts made it to a B cup and quit growing. I'd never be dainty, rendering me undateable in most adolescent circles. I was doomed. I found my place at the fringes, where the punks, the artists, the gypsies and the big kids hung out. After graduating from college, I hit the road, landed in the Canary Islands and stayed drunk for a year. It was probably the beer goggles, but I felt waiflike among my willowy Latina girlfriends as we danced the nights away then nursed our hangovers on sunny beaches.

On my 25th birthday, I awoke with a jolt to find myself face down on a dormant volcano with sand covering my little silk dress. I realized that if I was going to do anything with my life, it was now or never. My friend, Maria Jose, gave me a necklace at my going away party. It was a rune with the symbol for warrior on it. Because, she said, I was her Amazon warrior friend. She meant it warmly, not as a joke.

Sometimes I let my inner Viking shine. For example, I greatly enjoy belting out a lusty rendition of Happy Birthday in Norwegian for my

Photo: Joseph White

Katherina Audley

friends' birthdays. Once, when a friend turned 30, I wanted to do something special for her. I built a big hollow birthday cake and hid it in the backroom of the venue. I got naked, painted myself gold, put on a loincloth and a horned helmet, grabbed my sword, climbed into the cake, lit the candles and got wheeled out. Then I burst out of the cake and busted out the Norwegian birthday song. My friend loved it. A big hairy old man kept coming up and telling me I was spectacular but all of the normal sized men around my age maintained a safe distance. The women at the party wanted to dance with me and pose for pictures like I was a Disney character. But I wanted to be one of them, not their token Amazon warrior pet. Depressed, I went home.

When another friend begged me to jump out of a cake for her, I agreed. The trouble was, I had just started dating someone. He wasn't Viking sized and he didn't have an outsized personality. I outweighed him by 50 pounds. But he liked me! He really, really liked me. We were quite new and fresh. This time, "Flight of the Valkyries" was blaring as I was wheeled in. The cake was fancier. The candles were fierier. My sword was shinier and my helmet had real horns. Unfortunately, my new boyfriend looked at me like I was a big overbearing cartoon character. He dumped me a month later. He said that I should find a crazy artist to be with. I was too much for a "normal guy."

Being a big woman does have its advantages. While I know in my heart that I'm a lover, not a fighter, I also know that I could take most men in a fight if push came to shove. I am always left alone in clubs to dance while my delicate looking girlfriends are continuously harassed by drunken louts. The poor things leave their spots on the dance floor to huddle like a bunch of bunnies at the bar while the wolves surround them, leaving the floor to me and the gay boys.

I am blessed and cursed with a superabundance of energy and a lot of physical strength, for a girl. When I was a commercial fisherwoman in Alaska, I celebrated my power every day. I loved working myself down to the dregs ripping and tearing fish out of nets, throwing 10,000 pounds of fish from point A to point B, and manhandling all of those big heavy ropes. I felt like I was born for it and I knew a small girl would have had a hard time with that job.

I spent my late 20s in the San Francisco Bay Area, consecutively dating a trio of mild men: Ted, Tom and Tim. After the third one dumped me, saying I was just too much, I spent a week in bed in a muumuu, living on mint chip ice cream and pizza. That was the week I decided to give up on love and focus on work, art, friendships and family instead. The next five years passed without so much as a kiss. I got used to it.

But then, one spring, I visited a friend in Portland, Oregon. As I walked down Mississippi Avenue, big handsome men in flannel shirts with good haircuts smiled at me and said hello. Maybe it was just San Francisco that was the problem. Six months later, I moved. Before I even found an apartment in my new city, I took the plunge and posted a personals ad on Craigslist. My strategy was to tell them everything and show them a picture, so that they would know what they were getting into and not be disappointed or scared off when we met. I titled the ad, "Reluctant Valkyrie Ready for Love."

I got more than 1,000 responses. Portland loved my Vikingness. I felt like a rock star! I sifted through the emails until I reached the one from Joseph. He wrote that he sees beauty. He told me loves big, strong women and he backed it up with examples. He seemed to be all there. On our first date, he took me to the best restaurant in town, bought me an expensive steak and asked me questions about myself all night. After our first date, he read everything I'd written and wrote back with enthusiastic feedback. He got me. And so he *got* me. I think he fell in love with the idea of a reluctant Valkyrie before we even met. Then he stuck around to keep loving me even when I didn't have any love for myself. Inside of this love, I began to feel right in my skin. I can't believe I found him. It makes a huge difference, having one person in the world who believes in you and loves you completely. Maybe it's because I'm getting older and probably in large part because of Joseph, but I'm okay with being an Amazon these days, although Planet Tinkerbell continues to rub me the wrong way.

> "I may look like an ordinary mortal, but I am really a super scary, blindingly bright, deafeningly loud, dead sexy Viking goddess and I eat suckers like you for lunch."

In the spring of 2009, a friend sent me this help wanted ad: *Vikings Wanted: Tahoe Ski Resort Seeks Tall, Ruthless Scandinavians for Ad Campaign.* Applicants were instructed to send in a 60–90 second long video demonstrating why we should be the resort's chosen Viking representative. On movie making day, I rented a Viking getup and Joseph saw me for the first time in the outfit I look most natural in. He did not look at me like a panda on the loose. He looked proud and kind of horny. We spent the day rampaging quiet urban shopping areas, storming a fancy restaurant, pillaging my company's corporate headquarters and trashing an apartment. I got to eat a whole chicken with my bare hands, drive like a maniac and scare pedestrians. I was so happy.

The judges deemed me 96% Viking and I became the resort's official model. They flew me down, we did a photo shoot and I got paid good money to be big and loud. I was hoping the thing would take off and turn into more opportunities. But Ellen Degeneres never called. Neither did David Letterman. Never mind. It's good to be the person I am, which is Viking royalty, even if it is only in a little known three star resort during the off season.

These days, I carry my new Viking model identity around like a secret alias. When the IRS agents, the creepy panhandlers and the other bastards are getting me down, I remember who I am. And then I give them a look that says, "I may look like an ordinary mortal, but I am really a super scary, blindingly bright, deafeningly loud, dead sexy Viking goddess and I eat suckers like you for lunch, so back off." And they almost always do. And yes, sometimes I do wear my horns around the house.

Katherina Audley spent her youth hitchhiking around the United States and Canada. After receiving a degree in Ancient Religion from the University of California at Berkeley, Katherina traveled the world and now lives and writes in Portland, Oregon. Her work has been published in anthologies, magazines and online publications including Seal Press' *Greece: A Love Story*, *Voice Catcher* and 52PerfectDays.com.

Also Available from LaChance Publishing

LaChance Publishing's titles are available everywhere fine books are sold and directly from us at www.lachancepublishing.com.

Volume and institutional discounts are available.

The *Voices Of* Series

Packed with inspiring, informative true stories by individuals from all walks of life who have been touched by major illness, the *Voices Of* books are like support groups in book form. Each volume contains the latest medical information and a comprehensive Resources section for those seeking care.

"Poignant, insightful, moving… highly recommended."
Library Journal

Voices of Alcoholism

Voices of Alzheimer's

Voices of Autism

Voices of Bipolar Disorder

Voices of Breast Cancer

Voices of Caregiving

Voices of Lung Cancer

Voices of Multiple Sclerosis

Good Dogs Doing Good

Lives Transformed by Man's Best Friend

A delightful, heartwarming anthology of true stories that poignantly show how the humble dog continues to earn its nickname, "Man's best friend." Illustrated with beautiful photographs of the stories' canine stars.

"Will make you glad you have a dog, or wish you did."
Chicago Sun Times

Send Us Your Story

Do you have a story to tell? LaChance Publishing and The Healing Project publish four books a year of stories written by people like you. Have you or those you know been touched by life-threatening illness or chronic disease? Your story can give comfort, courage and strength to others who are going through what you have already faced.

Your story must inform, inspire, or teach others. Tell the story of how you or someone you know faced adversity; what you learned that would be important for others to know; how dealing with the disease strengthened or clarified your relationships or inspired positive changes in your life.

The easiest way to submit your story is to visit the LaChance Publishing website at www.lachancepublishing.com. There you will find guidelines for submitting your story online, or you may write to us at submissions@lachancepublishing.com. We look forward to reading your story!